DAVE HATCHER

SON OF THE
HEARTLAND

On The Way to The Promised Land

SON OF THE HEARTLAND:
On The Way to The Promised Land

ISBN (Paperback): 978-1-964494-79-1
ISBN (Ebook): 978-1-964494-80-7

PROMINENT
B O O K S
EDGE

5830 E 2nd St, Ste 7000 #9983
Casper, WY 82609
USA

TRAVELING TO THE PROMISED LAND

I found reading this book to be very interesting and because I am a West Point classmate of DAVID. It was also very personal. Dave has led a very adventures life, and I greatly respect his willingness to tell us how his faith journey began and is ongoing today.

—Gilbert Jacobs

Very Insightful

My friend Bob Whaley really enjoyed the book. A great expose on the experiences of a Midwesterner living in a different world.
Enjoyed it so much that he shared it and his experiences with his children
He highly recommends.

—JB

Impactful storytelling in this book about life and faith

An enjoyable read of Dave's life and journey of faith. I am reminded through this how God is faithful no matter how different the seasons of life may look and even in our times of spiritual wandering. This book is an excellent read about Dave's story and a reminder of the grace available to us in Jesus at all times!

—Matthew

Compelling & Thought Provoking

Dave Hatcher's autobiographical work, Son of The Hartland on The Way to The Promised Land is both a compelling and thought provoking read. Dave has eloquently sewn together the patchwork of a truly fascinating journey through life. To date, Dave's experiences have encompassed a robust spectrum of the globe, vocations, adventures, luminaries and family. Mid-life Dave took a hard right turn which causes one to ponder if the metaphor "It's not the destination, It's the journey" is correct. After reading his book, I'm in awe of Dave's life résumé but more importantly, I am contemplating my own destination.

—Tom Vollrath

DEDICATION

This first literary effort in book form is dedicated to those closest to me, most of all, my wife Vasana Chinbutr Hatcher. I could not accomplish this effort without the dedication from the family member closest to me: my spectacular, charming, and gracious wife of 42 years, Vasana, for her love, steadfast friendship, and good counsel all those years.

She would want to extend that dedication to our son Donnie, our daughter Vanessa and Vanessa's husband Scott and granddaughters, Elizabeth "Birdie" Poynter born in 2020 and Charlotte "Tippawan" Poynter born in 2022. I also dedicate this in memoriam to both parents, Claire and Don Hatcher, for their humble and godly example in all ways in my upbringing.

CONTENTS

FOREWORD

"The fool wanders; a wise man travels."

—Thomas Fuller

LIKE MANY OTHER young boys coming of age during the Baby Boom, I grew up wanting to be a professional baseball player. My lifelong hero was Stan The Man Musial of the St. Louis Cardinals.

But six years of Little League and Babe Ruth baseball convinced me that I had neither the right stuff nor the ability "to hit the curve ball, or the fast ball, or almost any other good pitch from another peer. I batted a stupendous (LOL) .194 one year in Little League: 7 hits in 36 at bats. Three of those hits included my only double and came in my breakout game! So, 4 hits in 32 at bats for an All-World average the rest of the season of .125. Very few scouts were interested in me, strangely enough!

All kidding aside, I enjoyed most of the traditional sports in the Heartland then: football, basketball, baseball, golf, and bowling. Some swimming and a very brief foray into ice hockey when our neighborhood baseball diamond was flooded in the winter. My impatience, however, in gaining the necessary ankle strength to just stand upright on the skates doomed any ability to skate, handle the puck, and avoid opponents.

I did enjoy one aspect of any game, however: running my mouth in a play-by-play account while shooting baskets in the back yard or pretending

I was taking the big shot, getting the big hit, or executing the winning play in one of the other sports.

Once enrolled at West Point, I began my love affair with lacrosse that lasted for several years, from intramural teams on campus to two lacrosse clubs after graduation, including three reunions since 1994.

As middle age dawned, I gravitated to jogging (two Marine Corps marathons in Washington, D.C. and lots of shorter races down to five-milers). I enjoyed piling up miles in many countries, not only in the U.S. but also in Thailand, Vietnam, India, Pakistan, Malaysia, Taiwan, Germany, France, Holland, Italy, Spain, and Austria). I have also detailed the great enjoyment I derived from several motorcycle tours in the Alps from 1979 to 2005.

My sampling of different sports and recreation mirrored my somewhat disjointed business and social career upon my graduation from West Point: a half-dozen years on active duty in the U.S. Army; nearly a decade as a foreign-based reporter; service in the federal government; and as a matchmaker for U.S. and Asian business partners in energy projects and infrastructure development.

I now realize that having an excellent long-term memory has allowed me to recall so many loosely-related personal experiences in such a "checkered past". I thank God every day for such a very good memory.

I always wondered if that memory trait originated in elementary school. My mother recalled a comment from my fifth-grade teacher during a PTA meeting. That wonderful teacher, Mrs. Wannerholm, told my mother, "David knows all the answers. I know he knows all the answers. I just wish that once in a while he would let others have a chance to show that one of them may know a few of the answers!"

After decades of procrastination, a 48-hour period in 2021 proved the catalyst for this memoir. There seemed to be a voice in my ear whispering, "Time to get serious." A few days prior, one of my two former roommates at West Point, Joe Mance, passed away in Paris, Kentucky from Agent Orange complications contracted fifty years earlier in South Vietnam. Joe and I actually overlapped in the same unit in Vietnam, but his exposure to Agent Orange came as a lieutenant. I arrived a few months later as a captain. I was not anywhere near where Joe apparently ingested the Agent Orange chemical herbicide.

Enroute to Joe's funeral, I hitched a ride with our other West Point roommate, Tom Vollrath. We spent hours in the car telling war stories, many of mine contained in this memoir. Tom often commented that I should memorialize many of those stories.

My daughter Vanessa also agreed.

> "Over the past several years, every time that my dad would recount personal and professional stories and memories with me, I would joke and say, 'You should write a book!' You can imagine my excitement when he finally decided to put ink to paper, and subsequently when Prominent Books Edge agreed to publish his memoirs. We look forward enthusiastically to the release of *Son of the Heartland*! And we sincerely hope that you will enjoy reading it."

This memoir is an attempt to dramatize one man's adult life, albeit an unusual one, hiccups and all. Oftentimes I acknowledge the sentiment expressed in the movie *Bonnie and Clyde*, when Warren Beatty rhetorically asks Faye Dunaway, "Ain't Life Grand?"

Yes, it is, but more than just grand. In a sad eulogy twenty years ago over one teen-ager's apparent suicide, a local preacher highlighted the salient points in anyone's life: "Life is a test. Life is fragile. Life is eternal."

We Christians believe that Life Is Eternal, and that eternal life has already begun, once we make our sincere request for forgiveness for our sins and acceptance known to Jesus Christ as Savior and Lord. As for me, "Surely goodness and mercy shall follow me all the days of my life, and I will dwell in the House of the Lord forever." Psalm 23:6

"The fool wanders; a wise man travels." I encourage you to be wise and not foolish—on your own way to the Promised Land.

#   #   #

ACKNOWLEDGMENTS

I AM INDEBTED to Vasana for all the love she has poured out on me since she first tried to escape my presence in her Volvo dealership office in Bangkok in 1980: our inside joke. She has been my best friend for almost 44 years of marriage. Till Death Do Us Part.

I profusely thank the networks of close friends, believers, prayer warriors, and fellow students in various Bible studies, not only for this book effort but for relationships with one or more with my family. Foremost of those close friends and their prayers might be all three components of our extended family: my side, my two sisters Carole Royther and Cathy Tikkanen; our son-in-law Scott Poynter's side; and members of my wife's family in Thailand and the US.

The advice from these family members has been invaluable. Just as invaluable have been the contributions and support from many wonderful friends: Phil and Kimiko Hannum, Tom and Sheryl Vollrath, Jane Peterson, Jack Bussa, John Wilkinson, David Hartman, and Mike Borschuk.

My optimism and good nature comes from the Scripture: "Rejoice in the Lord always, and again, I say, rejoice." Philippians 4:4.

# # #

CHAPTER 1

The Beginnings—Iowa, That's Where The Tall Corn Grows

IF THE BABY boom generation began in the year 1946, the author and "Son of the Heartland" was in the vanguard of that generation, born on the fifth day of February of that year. He became a man with a "checkered past" from his many life experiences as he matured during the second half of the twentieth century and into the twenty-first century. By way of reference, other 1946-year group folks include such American luminaries as Candace Bergen, Diane Keaton, Susan Sarandon, Steven Spielberg, Tommy Lee Jones, Sylvester Stallone, and Bill Clinton inter alia.

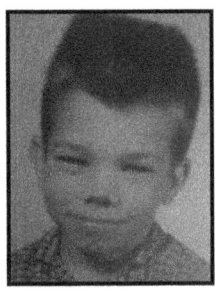

The author, Son of the Heartland, at age thirteen.

The author trying to watch Major League Baseball's
Game of the Week with announcers Dizzy Dean and
Buddy Blatner, holding his baby sister, 1954.

He breathed his first breaths at Lorain Hospital in Storm Lake, Iowa
and spent his childhood in two truly middle-class neighborhoods: the first
five years, including kindergarten, in the capital of Des Moines, and in the
Crescent Park neighborhood of Sioux City, Iowa, from first grade through
high school. Sioux City sits at the confluence of the Missouri and Big Sioux
Rivers and was known in the middle of the twentieth century as having one
of the largest agricultural stockyards in the country—before stockyards
gave way to private-industry packing plants. That agricultural marketplace
in the Heartland rivaled the daily numbers of cattle, pigs (hogs) and sheep
in stockyards in Chicago, Kansas City, Omaha, and Minneapolis.

He was truly a Son of the Heartland—with a prairie-girl mother born
in 1920 among the tumbleweeds of Deadwood, South Dakota, and a father
born in 1916 in What Cheer, Iowa, a tiny farm town an hour outside Iowa
City, the state's first capital.

What Cheer, Iowa, water tower.

Farms and small towns in that part of Iowa were positioned within a few miles of several colorfully named rivers that drained some of the world's richest farmland—rivers such as the Shell Rock, the Skunk, the Raccoon, and the Cedar, all eventually flowing into the Mississippi River, which separates Iowa from Illinois.

His two wraparound sisters, Carole the older and Cathy the younger, shared a good life with their brother in their Siouxland childhoods through Crescent Park Elementary School and the renowned Central High School in Sioux City, the Castle on the Hill.

# # #

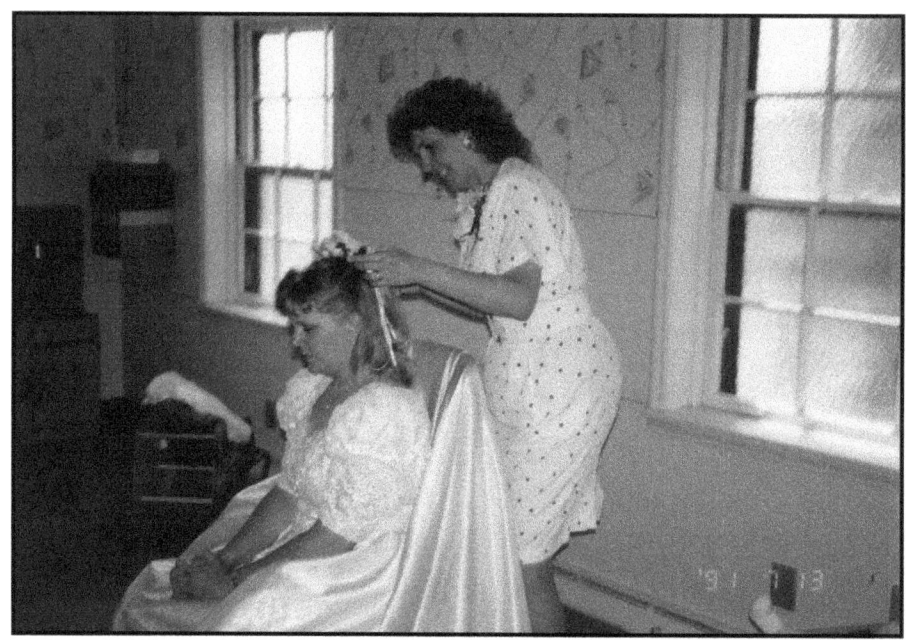

Sisters Carole and Cathy, Cathy's wedding, 1991.

CHAPTER 2

The Heartland and Roots in Iowa

THE HEARTLAND—GENERALLY THE greater Midwest from Arkansas, Missouri, and Kansas in the south to Nebraska and the Dakotas in the west and Tennessee and Kentucky in the southeast—cities like Indianapolis, Milwaukee, Columbus, Detroit, and the Twin Cities—along with Ohio River riverport towns such as Pittsburgh, Cincinnati, and Louisville before flowing into the Mighty Mississippi just outside St. Louis.

> "Those living in the Heartland weigh more and make less. They use more opioids and fewer of them are college educated … But when it comes to agriculture, the Heartland shines, producing more than the 31 other states (including California) and leading the country in exports." From "What Exactly is America's Heartland? A New Study Says It's 19 States" Doug Moore, October 18, 2018, www.sfgate.com

His father was a World War II navy veteran of the war in the Pacific who returned to Iowa to spend his adulthood working for a company selling highway construction equipment. The author was midway through kindergarten when the family moved to Sioux City, and their permanent address for the next four decades on West 28th Street—smack in the middle of a middle-class neighborhood in middle America.

Parents Don and Claire Hatcher, 1983.

My childhood years were not unlike those of seventy-eight million other baby boomers, many growing up in the Heartland. For me, I remember the excellent public schools and teachers, summers of Little League and Babe Ruth League baseball, many hot and humid afternoons at Leif Erikson swimming pool, and church, Sunday school, and Methodist Youth Fellowship (MYF) at the neighborhood Methodist church (that denomination merged with the Evangelical Brethren Church in 1968).

Drum section, American Legion Drum and Bugle Corps,
Sioux City, 1961.

One of the main social activities as a teenager was membership in the American Legion Drum and Bugle Corps in Sioux City. I learned to play snare drum with other teenagers who made up sections of drums, bugles, and color guard. (Our drum corps became co-ed during my high school years with the addition of teenage girls as flag carriers in our formations. I think one or two marriages resulted from that addition of girls.) Every summer we practiced our twelve-minute drill of music and marching religiously in the one or two evenings per week, leading up to the state American Legion annual convention every August. We competed against the Cedar Rapids Cadets, the Fort Dodge Lancers, and the Decorah Kilties. Besides practicing and performing annually in the state contest, we marched frequently on weekends, in some cases on weekdays, in many patriotic or special-occasion parades in Sioux City and in a variety of towns around the tri-state area. The tri-state area is so named for the states of Nebraska, South Dakota, and Iowa around the Missouri and the Big Sioux Rivers. The discipline of marching to music in a unit would become invaluable for my next life experience in a military school.

During my fifth-grade year at Crescent Park Elementary Public School, a dramatic anthology appeared on CBS television that changed my life. The series was titled simply *West Point* (not to be confused with *The West Point Story* motion picture of 1950 starring Jimmy Cagney, Doris Day, and Virginia Mayo). The TV series lasted only one year but ignited my dream to attend West Point and started me on a flow chart to qualify for admission. I was fortunate to do very well in the statewide Iowa Basic Skills tests for fifth and sixth graders (scoring higher both years than almost all other kids in Sioux City). In high school I studied Latin for two years and was enrolled in advanced algebra and trigonometry, among other subjects. I started writing letters to members in the Iowa congressional delegation in Washington. At the suggestion of my congressman's district office, I twice took the Civil Service Designating Examination. During senior year, I scored very high on my SAT and the ACT. I began a bi-weekly workout routine lifting weights under the direction of my private coach at the YMCA, Bill Carroll, a former US Army Ranger and veteran of World War II battles in Sicily and Italy. He had also given me swimming lessons a few summers earlier at the YMCA.

I was also active in several high school extracurricular activities. From track-and-field during the spring to the concert choir and the school marching band, plus Hi-Y boys group and, briefly in my sophomore year, to an after-hours program of Great Books (a study of the works of the trio of Socrates, Plato, and Aristotle—but quickly I concluded I could not "compete" with others smarter than me and dropped out). Our senior class elected me 1964 class president, with an administration of Stan Shrago, one of Central's top basketball players; Barbara Wecker, a gregarious and charming young lady; and Allen Johnson, a low-key friend to all and one of the top scholars in our class.

With that sparse high school record, I received a letter from US congressman Charles Hoeven during the winter of 1963 stating he was nominating me for a principal appointment to the US Military Academy—at

West Point, New York. A principal appointment meant I did not have to compete with any other candidates: if I passed my medical and physical aptitude exams during the spring of 1964, I would be accepted into the corps of cadets.

One unfortunate casualty of my excitement that winter was a leap I made over a small hedge at the home of a very close friend, Steve Jansen, to rush back to read the letter from Congressman Hoeven's office. I slipped on the ice in his family's gravel parking lot and ended up within an hour or so in the emergency room of St. Joseph's Hospital, receiving several stiches in my right knee to sew up the laceration caused by the jagged edges of the ice. (I immediately began to worry that the laceration might be a reason for disqualification on the physical aptitude and medical exams.)

A few dozen future USMA classmates from all around the Heartland excitedly came together for three days at Fort Leavenworth, Kansas that spring to take the medical and physical aptitude exams. (The eye exam involved having doctors dilate our pupils one morning. A few minutes later, we assembled outside for noontime mail call. All of us were forced to sheepishly shield our eyes like toddlers from the combination of dilated pupils and bright sunshine—hardly a "macho beginning" for future army officers!)

Within a few weeks, I received official notice of acceptance into the class of 1968, along with almost one thousand other similarly qualified young men. (West Point would not begin to accept women until 1975.)

Prior to leaving for West Point, I joined two dozen biology students for a postgraduation flora and fauna field trip to Isle Royale, Michigan. One of the last functions after returning home was the banquet. The event morphed into a surprise party for me at the same home of Steve Jansen, over whose hedge I had leaped for joy a few months earlier. I still have some of the toy weapons and kids' combat clothing as gag gifts from that surprise party.

On June 30, 1964, I boarded a United Airlines 707 in Omaha and landed a few hours later at JFK Airport. My mother said I had never looked smaller than I did climbing the steps to the doorway of the airliner. From

JFK I took buses to airline terminals in Manhattan and boarded the intercity bus from the Port Authority Bus Terminal to Highland Falls, New York, adjacent to West Point. I stayed overnight at a small guesthouse before walking through the front gate on July 1, 1964.

My journey from boyhood to manhood had begun.

Author on Christmas leave during Plebe Year, USMA, 1964.

CHAPTER 3

The West Point Years, 1964–1968

I STRETCHED THE truth for the next forty-seven months by saying I was doing time in a federal institution, but not Sing Sing (now Ossining) federal prison! From an incoming class of nearly one thousand cadets that first day, seven hundred and six of us graduated four years later, an attrition rate of about 30 percent. Our graduation day of June 5, 1968 will live forever in all our minds, not only for the attainment of diplomas and commissions as US Army second lieutenants but because it was the morning after the assassination in Los Angeles of then–presidential candidate Robert Kennedy. His assassination cast a pall over the formal ceremony and the shared experience among hundreds of families of my companions the last four years.

This chapter will not spend a great deal of time on a lengthy up-close-and-personal reminiscence of those forty-seven months but rather will generalize more memorable themes and impressions from such a lengthy and, tongue-in-cheek, federally sponsored incarceration.

My involuntary roommate thrown together with me that day was David Orr from southern California. Among other accomplishments during high school, he was a track star, recruited by West Point to compete on the varsity team in track-and-field. Once our two-month summer training ended, we were sent to different companies. We would hardly see each other during the rest of our "incarceration." I have long lost track of him. He may have decided to leave before graduation.

Our two-month first summer as plebes, called Beast Barracks, before all three upper classes returned for the start of the oncoming academic year, was an intense introduction to military discipline and performance under pressure. It was also an intentional effort to create the most level uniformity, a kind of lowest common denominator, to those military principles among a widely diverse group of young men.

Just like all other classes before and after, most of us came from high schools all around the country, with a handful of foreign cadets and relatively few cadets with prior college or prior military service. Throughout our plebe year, upperclassmen repeated ad nauseum the mantra for us to "cooperate to graduate"—admonishing us to make instant friendships among our plebe classmates, to enhance unit cohesion and reliance on others when needed.

We quickly learned to make our beds with hospital corners and blankets almost tight enough to bounce coins off! We pulled off our sheets and blankets weekly, folded the blankets and comforters on top of the mattress, and sent sheets and pillowcases to the huge laundry facility on-post, along with other clothing. To this day I make hospital corners of the top sheet at home, with the relative luxury of having fitted bottom sheets! But no inspection.

Labor Day weekend meant the return to post of virtually all upperclassmen except for those who had been our "training cadre" during the second month of Beast Barracks. We plebes looked on with great anxiety and apprehension as we stared out the windows before supper formation that first night, as great reunions ensued among the various upper classes. We had no idea of what we were in for, what the plebe academic year would bring, and the adjustment to the whims and demands of many of these upperclassmen. We were now separated by class year but often all together in frequent inspections throughout the day, from reveille to meal formations; to occasional weekday and Saturday parades; participation in athletics either intramural or intercollegiate; and the studying and homework from a large course load carried by all cadets.

I was placed into an advanced freshman mathematics class based on my high school SAT scores. I quickly became lost trying to understand the worlds of differential and integral calculus and statistics, barely making passing grades in mathematics the next two years. Other subjects played into this fast-paced immersion in such challenging college academics, combined with the military lifestyle we embraced with mixed emotions.

We attended class five and a half days each week. After Saturday morning classes, we often changed into full dress uniforms for the noontime parade before lunch. During football season, we made our way after the parade to Michie Stadium if Army had a home game that Saturday.

One of the few enjoyable pastimes a couple of evenings every week my last two years was being a disc jockey on our tiny local radio station, KDET. My classmate Jim Altemose was the cadet station manager and agreed to let me host a one-hour show. My disc jockey moniker was Hatchet Man. I used as my bumper theme every night the guitar solo "Apache" by Jordan Ingman—a sideways tribute to my upbringing out in the Midwest and in honor of the several Sioux tribes in the Dakotas and Nebraska and further west.

That's also when my love affair with the sound of Motown began: so many wonderful artists and so many great love songs by groups and individuals. One of my trademarks was to look through the top songs on *Variety* that week and see if I could play the current hit song back-to-back with a previous hit by the same group or singer.

Again, we had a very limited signal, maybe 50 watts. Our signal didn't go out over the air but through closed-circuit wiring into each of the several barracks buildings. We of course were hardly a rival for the rock powerhouses in New York City—such as WABC and WMCA—and the fairly new station WOR-FM, with its charismatic lineup including "Murray the K" Kaufman, Scott Muni, and "Rosco" (Bill Mercer).

I also grew to love and often imitate the patter of a variety of rock disc jockeys and their catchphrases, such as "Truly the Eighth Wonder of the World. Before me there was no other, after me there shall be no more!" "If I'm all you got, I'm all you need!" And signing off and signing on as the "Hatchet Man". We had no station ratings to see what the size of the listening audience was among the cadets studying in their rooms.

I valued the hour as a brief escape from the nightly rigors of home-work all of us carried. We averaged eighteen or twenty credit hours each semester—roughly 50 percent more than the load carried by most students in most civilian colleges and universities.

I did manage to graduate in the top 30 percent of our class and survived several fairly minor scrapes with tactical officers for some risky adventures. Many cadets going back to 1802 kept their sanity under the continuous, daily pressure from many directions. Virtually every day, it seemed there were commitments to meet: in academics, often including daily quizzes; military living and keeping uniforms and rooms in perfect shape; intramu-ral or intercollegiate sports; and living up to the occasional orders or com-mands from commissioned officers or upperclassmen, learning to "follow your last order first," when in doubt from conflicting priorities.

One of the two most infamous incidents occurred a few weeks before the Army-Navy football game in Philadelphia my junior year. My close friend Joe Henry and I had met two very mature high school girls from nearby Tarrytown early that fall. We squired them to social occasions on-post. Joe's date, Ellen, had a new Karmann Ghia sports car. On a very cold and blustery Saturday evening after an evening meal, the four of us, Joe, Ellen, and my date Marie, adjourned to the Hotel Thayer parking lot for serious late evening discussions inside the not-very-spacious Karmann Ghia. As Joe and I played smoochie-face with our dates, Ellen remarked that she thought there was someone walking down the line of parked cars with a flashlight. Not sensing any real danger, but realizing that Joe and I needed to be back in barracks before taps, we pulled out of the parking lot for the half mile drive to the cadet barracks. Within a few seconds of pulling out of the parking lot, we heard the sound of a powerful car engine following us. We pulled over and greeted the fellow carrying that flashlight. He was the assigned brigade duty officer that evening. He interrogated Joe and me and accused us of fleeing in the face of his desire to interview us while still in the parking lot.

This occurred the weekend before the Army-Navy game. Our reservations we had made for hotel rooms that weekend at the Ben Franklin Hotel in Philadelphia were canceled. The punishment for our "gross indiscretion in a public display of affection" came down. For that smoochie-face in an extremely dark parking lot with little other human life going on in the entire parking lot, Joe and I each received fifteen demerits; twenty-two hours walking "the area" in full uniform with M-14s shouldered; and one month in confinement, restricted to our rooms except for classes, meals, and athletics. We joined other cadets being punished, marching the hours off, two hours on Friday afternoons and three hours on Saturday afternoons. Our plans for the weekend went down in flames. We weren't allowed to leave the post, much less celebrate the decisive Army victory that year (we beat Navy 20–7). Ellen and Marie soon found better ways to spend their weekends and the rest of their lives in Tarrytown or anywhere not at West Point!

Joe Henry with Hatcher.

Another narrow escape from any punishment occurred after sophomore year, this time in Manhattan during our class's three-week June
Encampment summer training period. The one long weekend we were
allowed gave us a chance to let off steam—on a hot and humid Friday afternoon, three of us rode the bus into Midtown Manhattan—my long-term
roommate Joe Mance from Titusville, Florida; our close friend Jack Bussa
from Ladd, Illinois; and me. Given the stifling heat and humidity in the Big
Apple, Joe rushed to the small liquor store next to the bus terminal to purchase a pint of the cheapest Scotch whiskey the store featured. While in the
taxi carrying us to the New York Hilton a short distance away, Joe imbibed
a few quick gulps. Within a few minutes of being shown to our room, Joe
had finished the pint of Scotch and had fallen into a stupor. (The New York
Hilton offered deep discounts to West Point cadets: a double room went
for twelve dollars a night; if there was a third guest, the hotel staff put in an
army cot and charged another six dollars a night. Hard to beat a five-star
hotel in the heart of New York City for six dollars a guest per night!)

Joe Mance and Jack Bussa during impromptu
reunion in South Vietnam, 1971.

After cooling off for an hour or so, Jack and I roused Joe from his blissful stupor. We all agreed to walk to supper at the nearest Tad's Flaming Steaks on 7th Avenue. The price in 1966 for an eight-ounce New York strip steak, baked potato, and tossed saled, served in a cafeteria line, was $1.49 per customer—an increase of twenty cents from the 1964 price when, as plebes, we first learned about Tad's Flaming Steaks.

The three of us politely made it through the line, carried our trays to the back of the restaurant, and settled down at a vacant table for six. Within a few minutes, two middle-aged ladies came up carrying the same trays and asked if they might sit down at the other end of the table, to which the three of us agreed.

In breaking the ice, one of the ladies turned to us and said, "My, you look like very nice young men." (Our very short haircuts and unwrinkled shirts gave us away—compared to many other New Yorkers our age!) "Would one of you like my baked potato?"

Cue Joe as he roused from his solo happy hour a few hours earlier. Wielding his steak knife in a menacing way, he rose halfway out of his chair and bellowed, "No, but I'll take your steak!" He lunged awkwardly at the lady and her food tray. She of course let out a shrill cry as she stared into a possible serious wound. She jerked her tray away from the attacker. But she was just too slow. As the two ladies grabbed their trays and purses and scurried away, Joe was close enough to grab the lady's baked potato with his other hand!

Luckily, we had no military chaperones or any other good citizens nearby taking our names and threatening to turn us in, somehow.

Fast-forward to Joe's untimely death in 2021 from dormant Agent Orange damage acquired during his tour in Vietnam. Prior to that sad death, many classmates besides Jack and me frequently regaled Joe during scheduled or unscheduled reunions going back to that evening in 1966.

One memorable vignette that may shatter any "goody-two-shoes" image of a West Point cadet back then: the second of my two hardly egregious breaches of cadet discipline a few months before graduation, at the very fashionable New York Athletic Club (NYAC), again in Midtown Manhattan.

During my sophomore year, I just barely passed the audition (on the third try!) to join the West Point Glee Club. This became an extracurricular activity and frequent travel for concerts in many states and on TV shows such as *The Ed Sullivan Show*.

Every year back then the glee club gave an off-campus concert at the NYAC. A few days before the Saturday evening concert, Mike Glawe, an underclassman in our company, mentioned that his girlfriend had a friend in need of a boyfriend (no further information). Mike wondered if I would like to meet the same lady in Manhattan before the evening concert.

Mike said both girls were dressmaker's models employed by designers in the Garment District (and not to be confused with the stunning fashion models one sees on catwalks around the world). I said to myself, "How can I turn down the chance to meet a glamorous model? With no real downside and probably no exorbitant entertainment costs on a first date?" So, I asked Mike for the phone number of the girl and asked him to pass the message that I would call her early on Saturday afternoon to arrange to meet before the concert.

We had free time for a few hours after our afternoon rehearsal. I called the girl, whose first name was Pam, to arrange our get-together. She invited me to her apartment in Greenwich Village to meet a few of her friends. It turned out, when I showed up in her tiny loft apartment on West 13th Street, that the friends were three enlisted soldiers on leave from nearby Fort Dix, New Jersey. One of them was her high school friend from her hometown of North Platte, Nebraska; the other two were his army friends from Fort Dix.

For the next hour or so, a subtle macho contest of sorts ensued between her former friend (perhaps another old boyfriend) and me. She served me a first drink, Scotch and water, then a second, then a third, without any solid food to absorb some of the alcohol. Fortunately, before the alcohol had a chance to cloud my judgment, I realized I had to excuse myself and travel back by subway to the NYAC for the concert.

A minor calamity struck inside the subway car; the train lost power momentarily and stranded everyone underground with only emergency power for lighting. We were off again without a major delay to my exit and the short walk to the NYAC, to change into my dress uniform for the concert.

When I showed up in the backstage assembly room, my close friend and glee club president Jess Gatlin came over and asked me if I felt all right. Now why would he do that, unless I was showing some outward signs of discomfort? I assured him I was fine. The last-minute warm-ups soon were over, and we formed up onstage behind the curtain.

I am told that the next several minutes of the concert were a tour de force by yours truly, not from singing beautifully, but from several nonverbal gestures and gymnastics. The alcohol finally had kicked in and allowed me to perform a one-man display of unequaled body language. All of us seniors stood in the front row and wore uniforms adorned with large gold-and-black chevrons on our sleeves. I was to learn that for the next several minutes, while apparently managing to sing correctly, I was weaving back and forth, yawning between songs, and running my hands through my hair. While we were singing, no one else in the glee club was able to nudge me to straighten up.

Intermission ensued. We singers were free to mingle with anyone in the crowd. A close cadet friend, Stewart Beckley of New Rochelle, New York, had invited his mother, grandmother, and older sisters to the concert. Stewart often invited some of us to stay in New Rochelle during other performances in or close to New York City. I mingled easily with his family before we had to reform again for the second half of the concert.

Unbeknownst to me at the time, among the VIP guests were the commandant of cadets, Brigadier General Bernard Rogers, his wife, and the tactical officer who oversaw the Third Regiment, my regiment. That gentleman's name was Alexander Haig, who would later run for President and serve as Secretary of State before retirement.

General Alexander Haig, postretirement.

The concert ended without any other interruptions or bad behavior by Cadet Hatcher. By then it was too late to invite Pam out for a late-night meal. I excused myself over the phone, slept well, and returned with others to West Point on Sunday, without incident and without warning for what I would encounter Monday morning.

After our first class that morning, a message came to report immediately to the office of the commandant, General Rogers. When I reported, his first words to me were, "I want to know why I should not punish you for appearing to be intoxicated in a public place off-post at the New York Athletic Club Saturday evening!"

Ouch. Many ouches. Talk about a come-to-Jesus moment. I stuttered and dissembled about spending time before the concert with some new friends and having only a few social drinks but said I did not feel that I had been intoxicated in any way. Being a busy officer running day-to-day operations of the entire Corps of Cadets, he excused me and advised me to wait for the typewritten form that would be posted on our company bulletin board shortly requiring a formal written explanation from me.

I wrote my reclama to the best of my knowledge and without any blatant mistruths. For the next two days, I had enormous concern about the punishment I was expecting.

Colonel Haig came to my rescue. I will be eternally grateful he was in the crowd that night. He told me he had noticed my unusual "free expression" during the concert and had tasked his wife to shadow me during the intermission to judge my sobriety or lack thereof. Being oblivious to her surveillance, I carried on easily with the Beckleys. Mrs. Haig apparently formed the impression that I was just a bit relaxed during the first half of the concert but having a good time without any real impairment from alcohol or other substances.

Colonel Haig said that he and General Rogers, and the glee club director, Lieutenant Colonel William Schempf, had been in consultations about that evening. Colonel Haig said that the concern among the three of them was not so much whether I was intoxicated, but whether or not anyone else in the glee club might have been under the influence, slight or otherwise.

Colonel Haig also reviewed that my time at West Point had been largely satisfactory in academics and in military leadership, except for the incident the year before in the Karmann Ghia with classmate Joe Henry and our dates.

Colonel Haig and General Rogers were easily among the most professional officers I encountered at West Point. Both were Vietnam veterans, having returned the previous summer from command assignments in the Big Red One, the First Infantry Division.

The bottom line was that on that Friday, General Rogers called me back to his office. The three officers had been unable to determine whether others in the glee club may have had any alcohol in their systems. Rogers said he himself did not believe in punishing one person if others in the group may also have been responsible for similar behaviors or actions. So, the verdict: Hatcher wouldn't be punished!

My immediate reaction was overwhelming relief! I realized that a possible punishment might be what was imposed for similar egregious actions: a combination of twenty-two demerits, forty-four hours walking the area, and four months of confinement. If that were to be my punishment, the four months' confinement would take me up almost to the very day of graduation. I would be unable to see my parents at all for the several days leading up to graduation day, until the absolute last few hours at the academy.

So, the dropping of punishment meant I would be free to spend the few days of graduation week with my parents and younger sister. Everyone at West Point awoke that morning to the news that an assassin's bullet had killed John Kennedy's younger brother Robert the previous evening.

I pause to mention one other event that spring just before our graduation: the grand opening on *The Ed Sullivan Show* one Sunday evening of the new Madison Square Garden in downtown Manhattan. The grand opening on live television included not only the West Point Glee Club but also the movie star Barbara Eden (from *I Dream of Jeannie* fame) and, among other celebrities, an unknown female singer/dancer.

During rehearsals before the actual performance, none of us glee club members could identify the performer. Only during the actual live performance did we learn from Ed Sullivan himself, that the stunning and superbly talented young blonde was Joey Heatherton, a contemporary of most of us and the definition of a blonde bombshell and upcoming star of films and music. She traveled on many occasions with Bob Hope for his Christmas performances to American soldiers stationed in South Vietnam.

Our glee club performances allowed us to meet other famous personalities. We met Nancy Sinatra in 1966 on *The Ed Sullivan Show*, when she sang her famous hit "These Boots Are Made for Walkin'" (We all had semiprivate sessions in her dressing room where she signed copies of her publicity photo. She signed mine, "Hiya, Hatch!")

Other celebrities we rubbed shoulders with, either during glee club performances or during concerts at West Point, included Dinah Shore, Sammy Davis Jr., Dionne Warwick, and others I have forgotten.

Two postscripts from my professional relationships with Colonel Alex Haig and Brigadier General Rogers, which to this day demonstrated serious and sensitive leadership by both, especially General Rogers. By his extending of undeserved grace to me, and wise acceptance of the full details of the concert in Manhattan, I often told others that I would follow an officer like that in any situation, combat or otherwise, for his even-handed treatment and open-minded consideration of all factors.

The first postscript is that a few weeks after that fateful glee club concert, I had been rehearsing my role in a spoof of cadet life that every senior class presented roughly one hundred days before graduation, called *The Hundredth Night Show*. I had a significant comedy role in the short drama, but if I were confined until graduation, I would have had to drop out.

But I did perform, and right after the Thursday night full dress rehearsal, attended by many of the officers and wives, I was changing out of my stage clothes back into my cadet uniform, in a back dressing room somewhat isolated from the larger room that others in the show were using. Only one officer took the trouble to learn where he might be able to congratulate me on my performance that night: Brigadier General Rogers, who reinforced his leadership qualities by taking the trouble to locate that back dressing room and personally congratulate me for my supporting role.

The second postscript occurred at graduation—June 5, 1968. The graduation ceremony began beneath the bright morning sun over Michie Stadium and was attended by a few thousand family members of the graduating class, in addition to us graduates and the underclasses. My parents and younger sister were among the family members. Yes, we all took part in the iconic photographs of graduates throwing hats into the air when hearing the final words, "Class of 1968, you are dismissed!"

At that second auspicious event I referred to above—my graduation—when my name was called, the senior army officer presenting my diploma was Brigadier General Bernard Rogers.

Then–Brigadier General Bernard Rogers
presenting Dave's diploma, 1968.

USMA Graduation day, June 5, 1968, with
longtime roommate Joe Mance.

Our family spent three short days sightseeing in Manhattan, taking the Circle Tour riverboat around what tour operators say is the "center of civilization" one day. Dad and I dropped Mom and my younger sister Cathy off at Newark Airport the morning of travel, and the two of us set off on I-80 for Iowa. We stopped near Cleveland the first night, and then on the second day, we drove all the way to Sioux City.

# # #

CHAPTER 4

Lands Beyond the Heartland: Texas, Pennsylvania, Vietnam, Arizona, and Thailand, 1968–1974

MY GRADUATION LEAVE was uneventful. I visited grandparents in their tiny hometown of Nemaha, one hour east of Sioux City. I renewed acquaintances with lots of high school friends and others. I left for El Paso in early August and drove the first leg to Denver to see my older sister and her family before continuing to El Paso a few days later—a straight shot down I-25 through Colorado Springs and Raton in Colorado, then through Albuquerque and Truth or Consequences and Las Cruces (New Mexico, before arriving in El Paso.

The Officer Basic Course at Fort Bliss included several dozen classmates who had also chosen to serve in Air Defense Artillery (ADA) as their combat branch. ADA had been added to the other five combat arms branches offered to our graduating class: Armor, Field Artillery, Infantry, Corps of Engineers, and Signal Corps. The ADA basic course concentrated on the technical knowledge and likely duties of a second and first lieutenant and overarching subjects common to all new officers in the US Army. My West Point roommate Joe Mance and I selected our first assignments to serve together in the Nike Hercules missile defense unit guarding the Dallas–Fort Worth metropolitan area. But during the basic course, the army announced the closure of several Nike Hercules sites including Dallas-Fort Worth. Joe received orders diverting him to the Detroit site, and I to the Pittsburgh site.

Joe and I left El Paso heading east to Dallas as the first leg to join our respective official army units. I had friends in Dallas. Mr. and Mrs. Allen Early had opened their lovely home to me years earlier during a glee club trip to Dallas. Joe and I stayed with them for a couple of days before starting off on separate journeys to Detroit and Pittsburgh. My orders assigned me to the 31st Artillery Brigade headquarters outside Oakdale, Pennsylvania. After processing at brigade headquarters, I was quickly reassigned to the 3rd Battalion of the 1st Artillery, with battalion headquarters on the opposite side of Pittsburgh, in Irwin, Pennsylvania. After getting lost several times navigating the Orange Belt route from Oakdale, I reported to the battalion headquarters and was ushered into a brief courtesy call with the battalion commander. I reported the next morning to the Nike Hercules battery located near the town of Elrama, Pennsylvania, south of Clairton and McKeesport, Pennsylvania.

(Fast-forward to 1977. The town of Clairton was the fictional hometown of characters in the movie *The Deerhunter*—a movie in which yours truly had a cameo appearance on location in Bangkok, as a film extra alongside Robert De Niro, Christopher Walken, and others in a scene representing the streets of Saigon at the end of the Vietnam War. That scene is more fully explained later. But the movie shot in 1977 was almost a decade after my first assignment in 1968 to Pittsburgh.)

Poster of Robert De Niro from the movie *The Deerhunter*.

The actual Nike Hercules site was divided into two smaller sections a few hundred yards apart in the hills outside the tiny town of Elrama. When I arrived, the battery commander informed me that because of the downsizing of several Nike Hercules sites, he had a temporary surplus of lieutenants. The table of organization for unit personnel called for one platoon leader lieutenant for the fire direction platoon and one platoon leader lieutenant for the missile control platoon. My arrival meant an increase to three lieutenants in the fire direction platoon, two in the missile control platoon. I became the second assistant platoon leader behind Platoon Leader, 1st Lieutenant Joe Marino and the first assistant, 2nd Lieutenant Mac Williams. The missile control platoon leader was 1st Lieutenant Joe Lacher; his assistant was 2nd Lieutenant John Douglas.

Within a few months, the surplus disappeared with reassignments of lieutenants to other units. I was transferred back to brigade headquarters at Oakdale as the brigade safety officer and then given command of the headquarters and headquarters battery. The entire brigade staff, including all officers, were officially assigned to my command for administration purposes. The brigade commander was Brigadier General John Dean (of the same name but no relation to John Dean who was a political advisor in the Nixon administration and who rose to fame in Watergate a few years later).

Oakdale missile site, demo Nike-Hercules missile, 1LT Hatcher.

Being the battery commander meant daily management of the professional issues of the battery personnel, dealing too frequently with issues of money mismanagement and marital problems among newly married enlisted folks. One of the highlights of my Pittsburgh tour was my selection as one of four recent USMA graduates branch to speak to the class of 1970 during their senior year orientation at Fort Bliss—just like the orientation my class had received two years prior. Besides Fort Bliss, the tour included forty-eight-hour stopovers in Fort Knox (Armor), Fort Sill (Field Artillery), Fort Benning (Infantry), Fort Belvoir (Corps of Engineers), and Fort Monmouth (Signal Corps). I spent two full weeks in El Paso—the 1970 class had been split into two equal groups. I and the three other junior officers had personal time between both groups.

The presentations to the first half included a formal mixer at the officers' club. Cadets had the option of signing up beforehand for blind dates, or going stag. We junior officers stood in the receiving line alongside the Fort Bliss commander and his wife. This allowed us to get impressions of many ladies who had signed up for the blind dates. Among the ladies on the arm of her date was a tall and slender blonde in a stunning floor-length, tiger-striped formal dress in orange and green colors: breathtaking in every way. I made a mental note to locate her and ask her to dance. Her blind date was two years my junior. He could hardly object to an innocent invitation from a first lieutenant to dance with his date.

The stunning young lady, Cathie Christie, could easily have won any statewide beauty pageant. She agreed to the dance. I seized the opportunity to befriend her so I might see her during the next several days and escort her to the repeat mixer for the second half of the 1970 class. Her father was in the oil business with oil-drilling operations around Seguin, Texas, and family in El Paso. She was attending Southern Methodist University in Dallas but spending the summer with family.

I did not have a car while in El Paso. The looming issue, before the second half of the class of 1970 arrived, was transporting Cathie to the officers' club for the mixer. To the rescue came my close friend Joe Mance. He was on orders for Vietnam and was attending the six-week familiarization course on the combat vehicles being used in Vietnam.

He was gracious enough to lend me the use of his blue Corvette convertible for the evening. Lots of heads were turning at the officers' club that night when I showed up in a Corvette convertible with a beautiful young woman like Cathie!

Upon my return to Pittsburgh and subsequent assignment to Vietnam, the two of us had two long-distance dates. I visited her in Dallas one weekend, and she flew into Pittsburgh for a weekend visit soon after.

We lost contact until a chance meeting in 1988. Both of us had wed by then. My family and I were having supper one evening at Fuddruckers restaurant in Falls Church, Virginia. An attractive lady came up to me and asked if I was Dave Hatcher! Yes, Cathie, the same lady! Her husband was a lobbyist in Washington for a large Houston oil company. We shared a very, very brief reunion—twenty years after those first few days at Fort Bliss.

The other memorable incident during my time in Pittsburgh was my temporary assignment to assist a group of twenty-five foreign officers— most were general officers, air marshals, or admirals—from a handful of countries. They were attending a three-week defense management course at Carnegie-Mellon University, paid for by the Pentagon. Two army captains were assigned above me as the manager and deputy manager for the senior officers.

I was responsible for staffing the large hospitality suite in the chosen hotel for the two weeks in Pittsburgh. I also was responsible to draw per diem amounts for each officer from the brigade headquarters in Oakdale and pay each foreign officer. The officers came from Saudi Arabia, Argentina, Thailand, Philippines, Turkey, South Korea, and Iran (remember the year was 1969, ten years before the Iranian revolution). At least one of the three escort officers needed to be available in the suite during the evenings and overnight. I was also given per diem funds for meals and incidentals, so it was a very comfortable arrangement for those two weeks, notwithstanding the three round trips I had to make from downtown Pittsburgh to Oakdale to pick up per diem funds for the foreign officers.

Additionally in Pittsburgh, I was able to renew my love for lacrosse. I played midfield in the 1969 season and part of the 1970 season for the Pittsburgh Lacrosse Club. We played club teams and college teams and traveled to State College one Saturday to play Penn State University's team.

Pittsburgh Lacrosse Club, 1969.

Change of command ceremony, Oakdale, Pennsylvania, 1970.

I processed out of the missile brigade in the spring of 1970 and reported back to Fort Bliss to enroll in the same Vietnam familiarization course that Joe Mance had taken a year earlier. Six weeks later, I flew out to San Francisco to report to Travis Air Force Base for military air transportation to South Vietnam. Our chartered flight made refueling stops in Hawaii and Guam before landing at Bien Hoa Air Base in South Vietnam. The short bus ride to the replacement battalion at Long Binh was uneventful, but the completely new sights and smells of this tropical climate dominated my first exposure to Asia. The officers were housed in separate barracks from the enlisted men. We were instructed to wait until escorts arrived from our assigned units to transport us to those units.

Newly promoted Hatcher in arrival photo, South Vietnam, 1970.

Fortunately, the battalion headquarters of my new unit, the 5th Battalion (AW) (SP) 2nd Artillery was near the village of HoNai and on the other side of the sprawling Long Binh base, the giant storehouse for untold millions of dollars' worth of materiel always coming into that part of South Vietnam for the war effort.

Upon arriving at the battalion personnel office, I saw an unexpected friendly face from our hometown of Sioux City, Iowa: Bill Burrows. He and I belonged to the American Legion drum and bugle corps as teenagers. We saw each other frequently during my first few months on the battalion compound where I was assigned as the maintenance officer.

The battalion had four batteries, each containing about a hundred men. They operated twin 40mm antiaircraft guns. Each pair was mounted on a lightly armored chassis of the M41 tank produced from 1951 to 1954. The army designated the combat vehicle as the M42. Manufacturing the M42 occurred from 1952 to 1960; the combat vehicle was kept in service until 1988. Instead of being used as a lethal antiaircraft weapon, the M42 was used as firepower support with medium armor protection for ground support missions: convoy security along the highways; engineer work parties in rural areas; static security, especially at night, guarding fixed artillery positions and manpower stationed on fire bases around our area of operations; and related types of missions with other types of combat or combat support vehicles. Some soldiers called the vehicles Fire Dragons. I don't recall hearing that nickname used.

The battalion also possessed one battery of Quad-50 machine guns, four .50 caliber machine guns in a lightly armored steel cabin surrounding one gunner. The entire cockpit was mounted in the bed of an armored five-ton utility truck. The two differences between the Quad-50 and the M42 Duster were the Quad-50's very high rate of fire and the "whispering" nature of the projectiles, compared to the louder noise and slower rate of fire by the M42. The nickname for the Quad-50 was Whispering Death. The weapon undoubtedly lived up to its name.

As the new maintenance officer, I was responsible for helping units manage the regular maintenance of all vehicles and replacement of spare parts as needed, for the two types of combat vehicles and another unit of powerful searchlights mounted on the ubiquitous quarter-ton jeeps.

I immediately realized I would have to depend almost entirely at first on the chief warrant officer, who was the maintenance expert on all the vehicles and spare parts requistions, etc. His name was Norman Silver, and he came by his nickname naturally: the Silver Chief. And he was a superb chief, to my great benefit. He was patient and helpful in reading me into issues that our motor section in the battalion headquarters handled.

The most serious issue that Chief Silver identified was the very high usage rate of the large battery packs on the M42. One day I traveled with my supply officer colleague to Long Binh, carrying all sorts of spare parts requisitions. Our battalion had requested more than two dozen such battery packs. The supply clerk had only two on hand; the remainder would be provided when new batteries arrived.

The instructors at Fort Bliss had mentioned that one of the major maintenance problems with the battery packs was that they were located in the bowels of the M42. To reach the battery pack for any reason, the soldier had to lay down in the empty chamber on one side of the vehicle's interior and move headfirst a few feet toward the rear of the vehicle. It was understandable that too often, the physical movements to check the battery packs were difficult, so the frequent checks were ignored. If the battery commander or maintenance inspector of any rank were known to perform the same check, all was satisfactory. What was not checked often enough was susceptible to breaking down in the tropical environment and mechanical systems inside the M42.

The check needed to determine the presence of any pool of watery liquid that might seep inside and disable the battery. Unless this fluid was wiped off frequently, the vehicle was too often deadlined.

An M42 in a static perimeter defense of an aritillery fire base might not have a problem. Once the vehicle needed to be ordered onto any mobile mission of any kind, such vehicles were subject to stalling out.

So Chief Silver suggested that on my maintenance visits throughout our large area of operations, I occasionally crawl back inside the M42 to check the fluid accumulation if any. Not only did I follow his advice as maintenance officer, but I ensured I would continue the spot-check often as a battery commander within a few months.

That little task, with just minor discomfort each time, proved the miracle cure for sustaining much longer battery life.

I lobbied for battery command in my introductory call with the battalion commander. He made good, as noted earlier, when he gave me command of Delta Battery after a few months as the battalion maintenance officer. Delta Battery headquarters was in a small fortified compound in the provincial capital of Xuan Loc, roughly an hour east of Long Binh along a very busy highway. Both Xuan Loc and the village of HoNai near Long Binh had interesting histories. HoNai had been settled by North Vietnamese civilians wanting no part of Communism and fleeing to South Vietnam after the 1954 agreement that divided the country in two. A strong anti-Communist sentiment existed in the village.

Battery commander, Captain Hatcher, near Xuan Loc, Vietnam, 1970.

For South Vietnam, the provincial capital of Xuan Loc was the metaphorical second bookend with the village of Ho Nai. Four years after my departure from Vietnam, Xuan Loc became the site of one of the last heroic efforts against the North Vietnamese Army's advance on Saigon in 1975. The ARVN 18th Infantry Division, plus reinforcements, held out for twelve days during the middle of April, less than two weeks before the fall of Saigon on April 30 of that year.

Captain Hatcher inside armored personnel carrier after overnight operation with 11th Armored Cavalry Regiment, 1971.

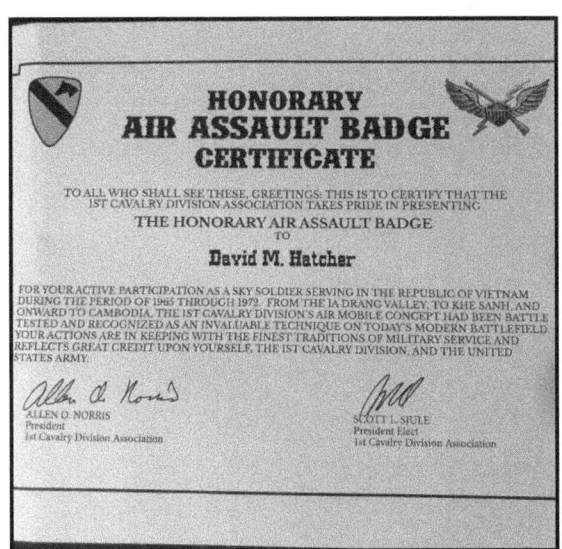

Honorary certificate, Air Assault Badge, 1st Cavalry Division.

Three different experiences during my command of Delta Battery form important memories. Two soldiers under my command tragically lost their lives—neither, however, from armed conflict. Both were junior enlisted men. One was thought to have died from an overdose of contraband heroin after returning from R&R; the second soldier committed suicide in his small sleeping space on one of the firebases where his crew was stationed. That sad loss was thought to have been the result of the soldier's continuous worries about returning to his childhood girlfriend in Louisiana, but possibly suffering major depression from an STD infection. As the battery commander for both, I had to write difficult letters of condolence to the next of kin.

I recall as a second lieutenant in Pitttsburgh, I had the assigned weekend duty once as next-of-kin (NOK) notification officer, requiring me to arrive at the soldier's home of record to deliver the very sad news to his family that their son had been killed in South Vietnam a few days prior. I remember the mother fainting within a few seconds of my quoting a telegram of great sympathy from the Army Secretary. I only served as NOK notification officer one time, and that was enough. It was very stressful.

The third experience during my Vietnam tour was much more enjoyable than these two sad occasions. Besides the seven-day R&R that was available to all military in-country, we were also eligible for seven days of regular leave, whenever schedules were conducive, before or after the R&R. I opted to take my seven-day leave first. Our battery was officially disbanded before I could take my R&R.

I decided to spend my seven days of leave in Hong Kong. The other eligible R&R locations at that time included Taipei, Honolulu, Bangkok, and Sydney, Australia.

I had no plans at all for the visit to Hong Kong. My first impression was the landing at the now-closed Kai Tak Airport. The descent into the airport between Kowloon and Hong Kong Island, separated by the bustling harbor in that former British colony, was breathtaking.

I ended up "hotel hopping" during six of the seven nights, staying in four different hotels. The shopping, to include tailor-made business suits and a cashmere overcoat, were among the delights, along with great international cuisine in a different restaurant every night. I practiced some financial self-discipline the last night, staying at the YMCA and watching the motion picture *Tora! Tora! Tora!* in a nearby theater.

Shopping was ubiquitous along Nathan Road in Kowloon and in the Central Business District on Hong Kong Island. But it was even easier to accomplish for anyone on R&R at the China Fleet Club, a six-story shopping mecca that housed all manner of shops selling a great variety of consumer products, to include all name brand 35mm SLR cameras, component stereo systems favored by nearly all of us, and high-quality ready-made men's and women's clothing and tailor shops. Persian carpets, sporting goods, household table settings and flatware, and other types of consumer products proliferated as well. The prices were greatly discounted in many cases, even beyond the prices on comparable products available through the AAFES catalogs. AAFES is the acronym for the worldwide Army and Air Force Exchange System with its global network of exchanges on army and air force installations.

The other two endearing memories revolved around sightseeing and two iconic eating places. The eateries were both on Hong Kong Island, iconic as much for their ambiance and decor as for the cuisine.

The first restaurant was the Peak Café, located at the summit of the funicular railroad from the Central Business District to the top of Victoria Peak. Its serene ambiance and romantic garden setting provided an idyllic midday location, for light meals or more filling sustenance. I fantasized about lingering over coffee with a modern day Suzie Wong from the 1960 movie with William Holden.

The second restaurant was the Verandah of the famous Repulse Bay Hotel. In 1971 it was the unparalleled resort hotel in all of Hong Kong. New owners demolished the hotel in 1982.

My visit to the Verandah included a special lunch with my former roommate Joe Mance. He was on R&R at the same time and had invited his American girlfriend to fly to Hong Kong. The lunch on the veranda, stretching the entire length of the facade of the hotel, allowed diners to look out over the manicured grounds leading down to the beach but afforded majestic views of the waters of the bay and several small islands and rocky outcroppings. An ongoing stream of passing Chinese junks and other small vessels plied the waters on this back side of Hong Kong Island. It was a very beautiful setting all the way around. I treated myself to one of its specialties, the expertly prepared pepper steak.

Upon my return from Hong Kong, someone in the battalion head-quarters alerted me to the official notice that our battalion was being dis-banded and all personnel transferred to other in-country units or allowed to rotate back to the US. We started closing down the operations of the battery, including recalling the M42 crews and all equipment; working with the battalion staff to help all the personnel get their orders for their next duty station or rotation to the US and possible end-of-service instructions; organizing a schedule of turn-in of all M42s and other vehicles; and clean-ing our barracks and office space for turnover to units or to the property management units at Long Binh.

The administrative tasks were performed without major incident. I requested a branch transfer from the Air Defense Artillery branch to the Military Intelligence branch and received orders to report to Fort Hua-chuca, Arizona, to enroll in the nine-month career course (or "advanced" course) of the MI branch.

Once back in the US and after a short home leave to see parents and both sisters, I reported to Fort Huachuca. I lived and studied on-post and became familiar with the desert topography and towns such as Sierra Vista (right outside the main gate); Tombstone (thirty to forty minutes by backroads from post); Tucson (slightly more than an hour from post); and smaller towns such as Bisbee and Benson. The Mexican border was within an hour or so by automobile. The two sister towns of Nogales along the border were a bit further away.

Tucson became a pleasant Friday evening outing for bachelors, who enjoyed the happy hours at Davis-Monthan Air Force Base. I occasionally stayed overnight with one or more former USMA classmates who were attending graduate school at the University of Arizona.

I also enjoyed spending weekends in Tombstone. For a short time, I dated the daughter of the mayor of Tombstone. I purchased a Honda 450 cc motorcycle prior to the start of the MI course. I enjoyed riding the back-roads to Tombstone and imbibing adult beverages in the town's famous bars near the legendary OK Corral featured in the 1957 movie.

During the nine-month course, we could apply for our next duty assignments and list our preferences on our dream sheet for the assignment officers in Washington to consider. The three preferences I selected in order of priority were Bangkok, Thailand, in the Joint US Military Assistance Group and US Military Assistance Command, Thailand (JUSMAG/USMACTHAI); second, the J-2 (Intelligence Section) at the US Pacific Command in Honolulu; and third, the J-2 section of the US Army Berlin Brigade in West Berlin, West Germany.

I received my first choice, the J-2 section at USMACTHAI in Bangkok. I had become interested in Asian cultures during my time in South Vietnam, apart from the war. I enjoyed learning some rudimentary phrases in the Vietnamese language and thought I would like to learn with greater depth the Thai language on an eighteen-month desk assignment at USMACTHAI. Both languages are tonal languages: several one-syllable words might sound very similar to the American or other Western ear but with different tones. Almost all new arrivals like me failed often with hilarious results to have my spoken Thai language understood by native speakers.

The Thai language has five different speaking tones for the same syllable: a normal tone, a rising tone, a high tone, a falling tone, and a low tone. My desk assignment was also to replace Art Volz, an army captain who remained there for three months before returning to the US. He was fluent in Thai as a graduate of the Defense Language Institute in Monterey, California. We worked together during the day and hung out or dined together often in the evenings. I also purchased the textbook *The Fundamentals of the Thai Language* by Stuart Campbell and Chuan Showings. My copy became indispensable in all aspects of reading and writing. Their comment on the tones: "Most newcomers to the language are rather appalled at the apparent difficulty of the tones but they are not as hard as generally imagined even for people with no musical ear."

When I arrived in Thailand, a different escort officer met me and took me to my first lodging, the Chao Phya Hotel that the American military leased for officers' temporary housing. Given the steady turnover of arriving and departing military officers, almost all of whom were either bachelors or on unaccompanied tours, it was commonplace for a complete stranger to be assigned to the same room. That happened on my arrival. I was joined for one night by an American naval officer heading back to the US from Diego Garcia island in the Indian Ocean. I stayed a few more nights without other roomates before moving into an apartment close to our JUSMAG/USMACTHAI compound.

On the second night in Bangkok, I decided to explore the streets outside the hotel and found myself in front of the Florida Hotel right across the street. It was a modest three-star hotel catering to American servicemen (especially enlisted men or noncommissioned soldiers) who were in similar transition modes.

The Florida was well-known for its Bora Bora Room on the penthouse level, featuring live entertainment that drew an eclectic mix of American men, Thais of both sexes, and assorted other expats based in the capital or living more permanently in town.

I was surprised and amused to observe the Filipino house band stop in the middle of a music set and direct all guests to climb the stairs to the rooftop and wait quietly until the "all clear" signal to allow customers to return to the nightclub. I learned that the local police frequently showed up unannounced to get estimated head counts of guests to judge the potential revenue being earned by the entertainment venue and adjust the business tax accordingly. Payoffs were not uncommon throughout many sectors of society, I was to learn.

More civilized inspections took place in restaurants. Staff in one medium-priced restaurant infrequently asked steady customers to stay away for a few nights. The management had been tipped off about the visit schedule by tax officers from the Ministry of Finance. Fewer diners observed in the restaurant for two or three evenings meant smaller revenues, ergo, smaller business taxes.

My duties in the J-2 Current Intelligence section were to monitor, using various classified sources, changes and trends in the country's Communist insurgency. I was the watch officer for the northeast region bordering Laos and Cambodia. At that time the insurgency was fairly young. It had begun in the northeast region in 1965 with Communist proselyting and aggressive recruiting among the rural population, modeled after Mao Tse Tung's jungle insurgency model in China and naturally deriving most of its support from China. Our office was responsible for weekly classified reports on the changes and trends to USCINCPAC and higher headquarters. Two other captains and I took turns giving classified briefings in the weekly staff meeting of most officers at the joint headquarters. The other two officers monitored the situation in the northern and southern parts of the country. Much of our information came from the debriefing of defectors, especially information on key Communist leaders and support details showing trends, large or small.

One of the most enjoyable ways of expanding my official duties presented itself soon after my arrival. Several years earlier, on an inspection trip in a very distant province, two officers—one Thai and one American—had sought refuge under the crumbling overhanging roof of a decrepit public school. Both officers decided to start a joint organization to raise money for improved school construction, or for repairing schools as needed.

The two officers came up with the idea to put on parachute demonstrations in a fun atmosphere on weekends around the country and coordinated between the Thai military and the Ministry of Education. Sufficient numbers of Thai military and paramilitary border police were parachute-qualified, as were sufficient American military stationed in country or visiting often on official business. One of those American units was the US Army's 46th Special Forces Company co-located with the Royal Thai Army Special Warfare Center in Lopburi, Thailand, approximately two hours north of Bangkok by paved highway.

By the time I arrived, the Mitrapab Educational Foundation—Mitrapab ("friendship") for short—was conducting demonstrations on a rotating schedule every year from February to June (the country's dry season).

Officers not parachute-qualified, and other Americans in Thailand—either in official capacity or from the Peace Corps or teachers at universities—could become qualified in a short course. Mine was taught by a US Army master parachutist, the late Colonel George Goetzke. He had more than 1,200 free-fall jumps, almost all being recreational, in his skydiving career. An enlisted man in our J-2 office, Allen Wilson, and I spent evenings at George's house and in his front yard, learning the basics of parachuting and practicing PLFs—parachute landing falls. When George thought we were ready for our first practice jump, he arranged for us to make our first jump out of the rear of a Royal Thai Air Force C-123 at Lopburi.

First parachute jump from Royal Thai Air Force
C-123, Lopburi, Thailand, 1973.

I had understandable butterflies inside the aircraft, pardon the pun. Once George ordered Allen and me to stand up and hook up our static lines (parachutists all over the US are familiar with the phrases) to wires inside the aircraft, I threw myself off the back deck of the aircraft, immediately turned around, assumed the classic free-fall position, and felt the jerk as my static line become taut, opening the parachute cover to allow the parachute to escape and fill with air.

The few minutes underneath a full canopy from about 3,000 feet was exhilarating, so much so that I wanted to go right back up and jump again! But Allen and I were through for the day and celebrated with "first jump" beers back in Bangkok.

George cleared me for participating in all the demonstrations in 1973 all around the country. Our routine on the weekends began with loading up at Don Muang Airport for the demonstration later that morning, with flight time to the province figured in. The number of jumpers varied each weekend. Included were not only in-country regulars of both militaries and civilians, but almost every weekend, qualified jumpers visiting Thailand on temporary duty from American forces elsewhere in Asia. One such group of qualified jumpers were US Air Force Combat Controllers who were crew members on the American C-130s that the US Air Force made available on weekends.

Each demonstration began with two jumpers, one Thai and one American, exiting the lead aircraft and carrying their respective country's flag. The two jumpers landed and presented the flags to the province governor on behalf of Mitrapab. The entire load of jumpers descended within minutes of the two flag jumpers. Most jumpers were static-line jumpers, leaving the aircraft as I described in my practice jump.

Several jumpers with free-fall experience usually jumped last during each demonstration. They owned their own parachutes, which were more colorful and had much greater aerial maneuverability than static-line parachutes—at that time, the MC 1-1 was the nomenclature for those standard parachutes.

Some of the free-fall parachutes were rectangular in shape and the earliest versions of highly maneuverable canopies. They were technically classified as "non-rigid gliders". They had a forward speed of up to ten miles per hour or so. The individual jumper could turn into the wind as he or she neared the ground and balance the wind speed in his face with the forward speed to literally come to a standstill in the air. Many times, he or she could just step onto the drop zone.

Informal photo of parachute group,
Mitrapab Educational Foundation, 1973.

A large lunch came next for the entire contingent and province officials. Oftentimes a soccer game between local teams took place to lend more festivity to that day's events.

The Sunday schedule mirrored Saturday's, with boarding and takeoff of the aircraft from whichever airfield was closest to that next province.

The unique fundraising of Mitrapab came from spectators who were charged a nominal amount of ten or fifteen cents in Thai currency. Sometimes crowds approached tens of thousands of spectators. At one such demonstration, local officials estimated the crowd to have exceeded one hundred thousand. For the great majority of villagers and farmers and all offspring, this marked the first time, perhaps the only time, that they might ever see Westerners in person.

One of the secondary goals of Mitrapab from the beginning was the psychological effect and advantage to the Royal Thai Government's anti-Communist strategy, especially in parts of the country where the insurgency was a key concern.

The Mitrapab Educational Foundation transferred the proceeds to the provincial governor for the construction of the new school or repair as needed. Mitrapab members traveled during the offseason to dedicate the schools where demonstrations had been held a few years earlier, and the new schools were already finished and operating.

For many of us who enjoyed the fun and athleticism involved, we also could engage in sport parachuting during the offseason, especially the cool season from November to February (the rainy season lasted from July to October). There were two locations for sport jumping. One was with the Special Forces soldiers and their Thai counterparts at Lopburi. On Saturday mornings some of us would drive the two hours to Lopburi for one or two or maybe even three sport jumps. Almost all those jumps were from Royal Thai Army Huey helicopters. The thrill of learning and practicing free-fall parachute jumps was just as great as the thrill from the first few static-line jumps.

I do remember one "cross-cultural exchange" at a sport parachute facility halfway between Bangkok and the resort of Pattaya Beach. I exited the small single-engine airplane without the best judgment either by the jumpmaster or myself. Once I began my free fall, I realized I had virtually no hope of landing anywhere within a hundred meters of the small drop zone.

I weighed my options and concluded that my safest destination was on the other side of the very busy Bangkok–Pattaya Beach highway. That side of the highway was covered with coconut palm trees and other vegetation surrounding rice farms or vegetable farms. I managed to slip through a small gap in the coconut trees and came crashing down right in a rice farmer's front yard. He was squatting outside his small home and was every bit as shocked and unprepared for the "cross-cultural exchange" as I was.

Fortunately, I suffered no broken bones or serious injuries, and did not damage the farmer's property in any way. Our team leader dispatched one of the jumpers to drive over to check my condition and transport me back to the drop zone. "All's well that ends well!"

My parachute logbook went missing years ago. To the best of my ability, I recorded more than seventy parachute jumps in eighteen months—approximately equally divided between static-line jumps and free-fall jumps. That pales in comparison to many friends, American and Thai, who accumulated hundreds or even thousands of jumps in years and years of activity. As I mentioned, when I met Colonel Goetzke, he had already made 1,200 sport jumps all around the USA and in other countries.

Plenty of lighthearted banter was ubiquitous with jumpers. My favorite was the one-liner: "Even with a total malfunction, it all feels great except for the last quarter of an inch!"

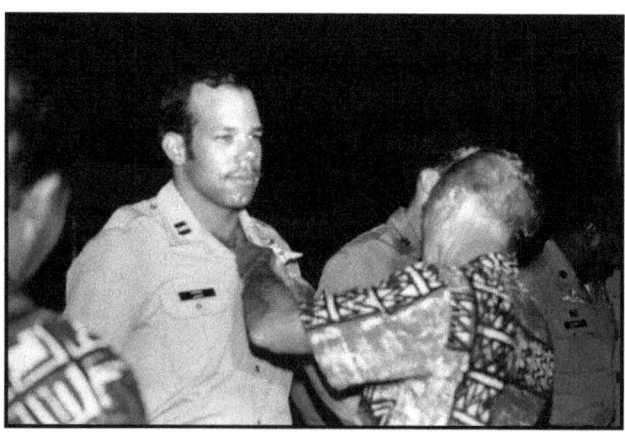

Hatcher being awarded Royal Thai Army parachute wings, 1973.

I was selected as the flag jumper for the first demonstration in 1974. Only a few more weeks remained before I signed out of JUSMAG/USMAC-THAI; returned to the US for formal separation from the US Army; and after a few weeks at home, drove to Madison, Wisconsin, to enroll in summer school at UW-Madison. I needed to make up undergraduate credits before my course load of graduate school began in September.

I would be remiss if I did not mention one other unusual aspect of my living conditions in Bangkok. Soon after my arrival in Bangkok in 1972, I moved to a three-bedroom, two-story colonial house just off the famous Sukhumvit Road. The house featured a long living room in front of the dining room and kitchen off to the one side. A back door led from the kitchen to the large garage and wide concrete parking area.

The long living room had furniture in a large regular seating area but left vacant space near the main entrance. I gravitated toward a unique conversation piece a few months later. I bought a round waterbed that was eight feet in diameter while visiting my sister's family in Denver. I had a carpenter in Bangkok build me a solid teak wood frame, with eight small sections attached together in a circular shape. The fit was perfect.

Not only was it a conversation piece but a great energy-saving sleeping location. The full waterbed and a simple rotating ceiling fan kept the water at a cool nighttime temperature. I needed only two bedsheets, no blankets. And no air-conditioning. The only trick to falling asleep was to sleep near enough the frame to hang one leg over and onto the floor, so that turning or tossing from the water jostling was kept to a minimum. I slept very, very comfortably almost every night.

Postscript: I don't remember how I disposed of the waterbed and frame when I left Bangkok. I may have offered both to another military officer or just left them in the house for the landlord to deal with.

And a second postscript: Twenty-three years later, on a business trip for an energy developer I describe elsewhere, I passed by the same house. To my surprise, it had been turned into a chic restaurant with seating for customers in the living and dining rooms and alfresco dining in the sizeable front yard! The restaurant owner was a young lady from southern Thailand—who knew nothing of that waterbed and custom-made teakwood frame.

# # #

CHAPTER 5

Leaving the Army for Graduate School in Ultra-Liberal Madison, Wisconsin, 1974–1976

"THE UNIVERSITY OF Wisconsin is 900 acres of university—surrounded by reality!" One of the slogans that was heard occasionally on campus.

While still in Bangkok and before submission of my resignation letter, I wrote to the army's career management office in Washington about attending graduate school as my next assignment. I was instructed to get accepted to a preferred university and advise the career management office. I did that over the next few weeks, providing my USMA transcripts to three institutions: Stanford University and the Universities of Missouri and Wisconsin. I received acceptance notices from all three.

The army informed me that the two state universities were still acceptable, but Stanford University had been removed from consideration because of changing policies at the university—with the army ROTC program.

That made my choice a bit easier for the simple reason of having family friends in Madison. Both universities shared excellent reputations for their departments in communication arts or broadcast journalism. Both were close to home in Iowa, and I could attend either university under the GI Bill with the federal government's discount for tuition. My parents had been close friends with another young married couple, all four with Iowa roots and all just out of high school or vocational school, in Des Moines. The other couple had moved to Madison some time before I was out of high school.

Another university I should have seriously considered was the University of Iowa. I would have saved a great deal of money paying in-state tuition and receiving the financial benefits from the GI Bill. Only after I enrolled at UW-Madison and started classes did some professors say the two universities were generally equal in quality of their graduate programs in that discipline.

My major professor for the course curriculum I selected was Dr. Larry Lichty, who would achieve national prominence for his role as a technical consultant in the production of several renowned documentaries on the Vietnam War. After some one-on-one consultations about my curriculum, and his teaching the main course during the twelve months of my three semesters of campus enrollment, he and I developed a strong friendship. He was intrigued with my military service in Southeast Asia and my academic maturity—compared to most graduate students who began their studies right after their bachelor's degrees.

Dr. Larry Lichty, PhD, major professor,
University of Wisconsin–Madison.

As my major professor, he oversaw my work on my master's degree thesis. After my relocation from Thailand to the US and to Falls Church, Virginia, we lived within a few miles of each other during his temporary position at the University of Maryland. Shortly after that, he accepted a professorship with full tenure in the school of communication at Northwestern University in Evanston, Illinois.

Three of the intertwined "good times" I had while in graduate school included a semester internship in the spring of 1975 at a Madison affiliate for ABC Television, WKOW-TV. I was an associate producer for the late-night news—at a time when the North Vietnamese Army was overrunning South Vietnam. I helped prepare stories for the late broadcasts, to include writing lead-ins and recommending video feeds to affiliates from ABC News. Many stories were dealing with ongoing developments in South Vietnam and Cambodia until late April when South Vietnam surrendered and Cambodia fell into the hands of the genocidal Khmer Rouge.

The second highlight and most fun I had was becoming a charter member on our lacrosse club team in its first year. An architect in Madison, Bruce Tully, was the founder/head coach. He started the club team without university affiliation; our team was called the Madison Gladiators. One of my close teammates that first year, Hal Rosenberg from New York City, went on to finish his schooling at the university and open up a successful private psychology practice in Madison.

Madison Gladiators Club Lacrosse Team, 1975.

Mini reunion with former Gladiator (Lacrosse) Hal Rosenberg, 2021.

Over the next several years Hal not only played every year but took on several roles to register the team with the university athletic department as a club sport—not a varsity sport, however. He still actively manages three different club teams under the university's auspices. (Other Big Ten schools that currently play varsity-level lacrosse include the University of Michigan, Ohio State, and for the last few years, with Big Ten expansion, Maryland, Rutgers, and Penn State.)

We lost every game our first year! In one game I found myself playing against a former All-American football player at Ohio State, Jim Stillwagon. He was an assistant football coach at OSU after graduation and was playing club lacrosse in the offseason. He was a great athlete but did not have very well-developed stick-handling skills, so he did not totally embarrass me on the field!

One other highlight of that lacrosse season was a weekend trip to Michigan. On Saturday we played a tiny college called Hillsdale College; on Sunday we played the University of Michigan club team in Ann Arbor.

I knew nothing at the time about Hillsdale College. Several years later a close friend gave me a subscription to its monthly speech digest called

Imprimis. The more I read those monthly issues, the more I became interested in the overall philosophy of the school—"Educating for Liberty and Freedom since 1844." Little did I know at the time but thirty years later, I would be able to place my daughter at Hillsdale and proudly celebrate her graduating cum laude in 2008. One of the current college fundraisers while my daughter was there told me that he remembered playing against our team that Saturday afternoon in 1975! Small world!

The third string during my time as a graduate student was my "learning on the job" being able to experience commercial broadcasting up close and personal, beyond the semester internship previously mentioned. Both such experiences occurred as "bookends" before and after my second year at Madison. Both took place in Iowa and not in Madison. After my first year, I was able to spend my summer at home, working full-time for two months at KTIV, one of the local TV stations in Sioux City. The station manager allowed me to spend time in several departments of the station's operations. One "lecture" I gave to employees, drawing upon my graduate courses in Madison, was a short explanation on program ratings and the differences between both major national ratings services, Nielsen and Arbitron.

I spent time with the sales department and worked in the news department. I even spliced my own 16mm news film to edit a few stories—before such splicing became obsolete with videotape and electronic news gathering.

The other bookend was the following year as a part-time reporter at another station in Sioux City, KCAU-TV, while finishing my master's degree thesis at home.

I spent two weeks that spring traveling back to Thailand to see some friends from my former military assignment and to survey the landscape of the international press corps in Bangkok. Many global news agencies had either moved their Southeast Asian bureaus from Saigon or increased what had been a smaller Bangkok office compared to Saigon.

Among the news agencies I visited was the newly established CBS News bureau and its crew, including correspondent Peter Collins, cameraman Kurt Hoefle, and soundman Derek Williams. With a stroke of good fortune, I suggested they do a story on the Mitrapab Educational Foundation by covering an upcoming parachute demonstration in a province close to Bangkok. Peter Collins had been parachute-qualified from previous army service, so the leaders of Mitrapab quickly approved having him participate in the jump and having Kurt and Derek document his landing with dozens of other jumpers. The story was visually appealing: the great variety of colors in uniforms, helmets, and airplanes; the pictures of dozens of parachutists floating down to the drop zone; and "perfect" close-up pictures of thousands of local Asians witnessing the demonstration.

CHAPTER 6

Back to Thailand and a New Adventure in Journalism, 1976–1984

WHEN I RETURNED to the US to complete my master's thesis, I was trying to decide what to do after finishing graduate school.

The few days in Bangkok allowed me to associate with foreign news crews, especially the CBS crew. The only other "communications" position back in the US that interested me was as an account executive and analyst with either Arbitron or Nielsen. I decided against pursuing either potential opportunity. A job in Chicago with either ratings service may have come with a sizeable salary, whereas a decision to show up in Bangkok as a "new face" breaking in as a foreign reporter offered no reliable salary of any amount.

What may have closed the deal was the current international scene at that time: the fall of Saigon and South Vietnam a year earlier; Communist victors taking over in neighboring Cambodia and Laos; my exposure to the general nature of geopolitics in Southeast Asia, and a rudimentary knowledge of the Thai language.

I received a letter from Peter Collins saying how much the three of them appreciated my help in the Mitrapab story and wished me well in finishing my thesis and my decision on the future. Peter said he would recommend to CBS News in New York that they consider sending me to Bangkok as a CBS radio stringer if I had any interest.

From there, the decision solidified. I recorded and submitted two or three notional news stories on regional developments to the CBS radio desk in New York, just to give producers there some idea of my writing and my broadcast delivery.

I sold what furniture and household goods I had. I needed the profits from that sale for early cash flow once in Bangkok. A close friend from my days at the local TV station the year before agreed to travel with me for two weeks. We had vague plans to explore a long-distance business opportunity importing precious jewelry from Thailand to sell to retail outlets in the tri-state area of Iowa, Nebraska, and South Dakota, and perhaps beyond. One of my close Thai friends was a key supporting member of Mitrapab and had a flourishing business exporting 14K and 18K fine gold jewelry to fashionable jewelry stores and jewelry chains in Europe, Japan, and the US. Our plan to exploit the key connections did not survive much beyond the friend's two weeks in Thailand. He returned to his full-time sales job at the TV station; I had no incoming orders from him for our trusted supplier; and I had my own priorities struggling to become known with CBS News in New York, Bangkok and the Asia bureau in Hong Kong.

The regional political tension was increasing. I started to adjust myself to the routines of a reporter, especially developing news sources among embassy diplomats; government and military offices in Bangkok; the regional UN office and numerous other international organizations; and refugee relief organizations, for example.

In the year and a half since the climactic downfall of South Vietnam, Cambodia, and Laos, the situation in Thailand, especially in the northeast provinces bordering Cambodia and Laos, had worsened. There were fears that Thailand would in fact be the next "domino" in the domino theory of countries in mainland Southeast Asia succumbing to Communist takeovers like so many fallen dominoes.

Leftist students at one of the two largest universities in Bangkok had started a nonviolent protest movement against the civilian-led government in Bangkok. The Thai military and security establishment assumed a higher state of readiness, fearing more internal upheaval from the Communist takeovers in Thailand's neighbors. Shortly after my arrival in Bangkok in August, student protests at the famous *Sanam Luang* ("Central Park") adjacent to the university and close to the most sacred Buddhist temples in Thailand increased in frequency and passion. Some of the rallies included loudspeakers broadcasting *The Internationale*—the standard anthem of the socialist/Marxist movement since the late 1800s.

On the morning of October 6, 1976, a date no Thai adult at the time will ever forget, elements of the Royal Thai Border Patrol Police and groups of farmers and peasants loyal to the monarchy launched a heavily armed invasion of Thammasat University, where student protestors had taken to sleeping outdoors in the huge courtyard. The proximate cause for the attack was a potential *lèse-majesté* incident a few days earlier showing a life-sized effigy of the Thai crown prince being hanged. The implication was that the student protestors had publiized the incendiary photo of the incident. No one ever admitted to being responsible, and rumors abounded that some elements within the security establishment had staged the incident in a false flag operation.

Regardless, the grounds of the university and the driveway entrances became one chaotic battleground. Our crew and numerous other news crews and reporters had received early warning notices that morning and were in place to witness the horrific bloodletting as the Thai BPP and armed civilians engaged in numerous acts of violence and killing. Our CBS crew waded into the main driveway and were engulfed in a sea of students, angry anti-leftist civilians, and BPP units. I personally witnessed, while cameraman Kurt Hoefle and soundman Derek Williams recorded, the brutal killing of one student trying to escape, but the simple density of the crowd forced him to stop in the driveway. He was beaten to death by someone using a folding metal chair. Many other scenes of unbelievable violence occurred in the driveway, on the streets alongside the university, and on the grounds inside.

The attacks continued into the early evening. Some students suffered being "necklaced" with burning tires, their burned corpses hanging from trees bordering the park grounds. The government forbade local newspapers from publishing all photos.

Thammasat University student hanged during riots, 1976.

One Thai photographer working for UPI was wounded in the neck by a stray bullet while he was standing close to our news crew in the same driveway.

Nightfall came. Announcements over all radio and television stations said that the Royal Thai Armed Forces were assuming control of the country to stop the bloodshed. Hundreds of leftist students managed to survive the onslaught but were apprehended and shipped off to military posts outside Bangkok to unknown fates. I filmed dozens of terror-stricken students who were crawling on hands and knees behind the university grounds to escape by diving into the Chao Phya River.

There was obviously no way that any of the foreign television crews would get permission to transmit such shocking satellite footage from Thailand. The three American television crews had always relied on the fallback option of sending heavy-duty reinforced string bags containing undeveloped film reels and recorded narrations to Hong Kong via passengers willing to hand-carry the materials on that evening's last flight from Bangkok.

Political life in Thailand changed radically overnight and for the next several years as the Thai military strengthened its grip on all government institutions. And not only in Thailand but in the neighboring countries. Thailand would have to cope with hundreds of thousands of refugees from all three neighboring countries. The post–Vietnam War regional landscape was changing to include the refugee crisis dynamic.

The bottom line of that political violence in Thailand within two months of my arrival: a not-so-gradual way to be welcomed into the world of foreign reporting in the tropics.

As I have mentioned, many international news agencies had relocated from Saigon or had enlarged their Bangkok offices. One of the best ways to start to develop contacts and sources was by joining the Foreign Correspondents' Club of Thailand. The club was seeing expanded membership from newly arriving reporters and producers from AP, UPI, AFP, Reuters, Deutsche Presse, Japanese newspapers and television news media, and many other large newspapers and radio/television agencies from many countries.

Even Tass and Pravda had correspondents in Bangkok who belonged to the FCCT. The Tass correspondent at the time was Alexander Polyanski. Press attachés in some of the big embassies and fellow journalists liked to say that Polyanski was an identified GRU intelligence agent. My own interaction with him was always superficial.

He enjoyed telling anti-Chinese jokes, including one about the three political prisoners languishing in a Beijing prison. The first prisoner asked the second prisoner, "What are you in jail for?" The second prisoner replied, "I was an opponent of Deng Xiaoping." The second prisoner turned to the first and asked the same question, to which the first prisoner replied, "I was a supporter of Deng Xiaoping." Then the two prisoners asked the third cellmate why he was there. He replied, "I'm Deng Xiaoping."

Within a year or so, Alexei's headquarters in Moscow relayed to him that their biographic research on me had uncovered my intelligence assignment a few years earlier to JUSMAG/USMACTHAI. From then on, he always smirked when he called me "Captain Hatcher." I smiled and dismissed his cute revelation.

At other times, in Bangkok, Alexei would hint that my intelligence assignment indicated that I may still be getting paid by one of the American or British intelligence agencies. I always answered in a good-humored and truthful way that none of my bank accounts anywhere would show any such deposits.

The FCCT accepted not only full-time reporters and news agency staffs as full members but also accepted associate members, i.e., any other residents, both expatriates and Thai citizens; frequent visitors who were a mix of businesspeople; embassy diplomats and military attachés; staff of international nongovernment organizations; and Thai government officials and top levels of the Thai military.

A very eclectic group, mostly expatriates, almost all of whom had some scholarly or professional interest in the changing geopolitical situation in Southeast Asia. The FCCT sponsored weekly programs of academic or sociological interest for members in addition to ensuring a comfortable club environment in the confines of four successive top hotels (Oriental, Montien, President, and Dusit Thani) before opening its own premises. Lo and behold, I would become FCCT president in 1981 for one year.

International stories in the region percolated for several months without any major events after the October 1976 bloodletting. One of the unusual diversions that many expats took advantage of the following year was the call for extras for the filming of the movie *The Deerhunter* starring Robert De Niro, Meryl Streep, and Christopher Walken. American film producers were beginning to make Vietnam War movies and to use Thailand (along with the Philippines) for scenes in Vietnam. The American producers had hired a close Thai friend to gain government permission for filming in many parts of the country. Through him I signed up as a male extra for the scenes featuring American soldiers.

My tiny claim to stardom came in one of the evening scenes supposedly on the popular Tu Do ("Liberty") Street in Saigon. Before the war's end, the street had several bars catering to the American soldiers. In the movie, the evening scene opens with a long overhead shot of the street jammed with all sorts of conveyances and pedestrians, attempting to show the chaotic lives of many South Vietnamese as the North Vietnamese Army closed in on the capital.

Christopher Walken's character begins to walk toward the camera among all the commotion, in hopes of locating his best friend, played by Robert De Niro. In the front of the scene, there is a scuffle showing three American soldiers struggling with each other. The camera briefly zooms in and shows two Army MPs trying to restrain and take away an intoxicated soldier who is doing all he can to free himself. The actor brilliantly playing the inebriated soldier is yours truly!

Knowing that the camera would dwell ever so briefly on this struggle, I did my best to use all manner of body contortions, with my face to the camera as much as possible. Viewers now have to look very quickly, once that scene starts to see, much less recognize, the brilliant actor playing the drunken soldier resisting arrest. I have obviously repeated that true story many, many times.

The two MPs were played by two very close friends: New Zealand native John McBeth, whse daytime job was as a respected reporter for the Asian newsmagazine *The Far Eastern Economic Review*, and Dr. Dick Graham, from Alliance, Nebraska, by way of the University of Nebraska Dental School, and active-duty service in the US Army in Thailand as a dentist serving active-duty American military and dependents.

Both would agree a few years later to participate in my wedding, Dick as my best man and John as a groomsman and usher.

Dick Graham, top, and John McBeth, below, Raft Trip in Thailand, 1980.

All extras were paid the sum of thirty-five dollars any day we were on call.

After the aforementioned scene, the film shows Christopher Walken entering one of the bars to look for De Niro. My close friend Dr. Graham was chosen as one of the extras occupying one of the barstools. During the rehearsals and several takes of the scene, all the extras in the bar had their drinks refreshed with actual alcohol. To this day, Dr. Graham says he cannot remember when Oscar-winning film director Michael Cimino shouted "Cut!" followed by "That's a wrap," or words to that effect.

In a way, the filming effort highlighted the looming refugee crisis as thousands of refugees began to strain the resources of the Thai government, among other neighbors. Refugees streaming out of Laos, Cambodia, and South Vietnam became magnets drawing many international refugee and relief organizations to Bangkok. The crisis became a big international story in many ways, mostly because of the legacies of the Indochina War.

Within a few weeks of the filming and life returning to normal, the Asia bureau chief for *Newsweek* based in Hong Kong walked into our CBS office and asked me to become the *Newsweek* stringer just like my stringer status with CBS News (and soon to be with the BBC).

That *Newsweek* bureau chief was Holger Jensen. He was very well-known to many former Saigon-based colleagues for friendships and travails covering the fighting in Vietnam, Cambodia, and Laos. Like many, Holger was a memorable character. He was born to expat parents in China before the Communist revolution. His Danish father managed a dairy in Shanghai. His mother was ethnic Russian. (I never learned about the circumstances of the wedding of Holger's parents.)

The family was forced to flee after the Communist takeover. Holger came to love his formative years in the family's new home in South Africa. He loved the outdoors, becoming an experienced deep-sea fisherman and wild game hunter.

Holger Jensen, Hong Kong bureau chief, *Newsweek* magazine, 1978.

I mention Holger's name not only as one of my mentors and close supervisors but also for his favorite memory of requesting reimbursement for expenses when covering a story. On one occasion with the Associated Press he was assigned to cover a story in southwest Africa before it became Namibia. He was driving a rented Land Rover along a deserted road when he came upon a "warthog migration" of thousands of adult and juvenile warthogs crossing the road. He was forced to wait in the Land Rover until all the warthogs had crossed the road. When he stepped outside, he realized that the crush of the enormous migration had scraped all the paint off the fenders in nearly a perfect straight line up to the lower half of the door panels around the entire car—completely down to the steel chassis.

He submitted a claim for reimbursement for repainting the Land Rover. The accountants back in New York refused his warthog migration claim and thought that Holger was merely trying to seek easy money from the AP. Undaunted, Holger submitted the same claim in the next month's expense reporting; the claim was denied.

Without missing a beat, Holger accepted his defeat but advised the accountant staff back in New York that he would ultimately manage to extract the claimed amount for the repainting. Over the next several months, he added small amounts to several unidentified legitimate expenses until his claim was paid without the accountants' realization.

Holger would become a very sympathetic endorser of my monthly expense reports for *Newsweek* until his reassignment from Asia within a few years.

# # #

CHAPTER 7

Two Holidays Outside of Thailand: Nepal, Europe, and the USA, 1978

I WAS FORTUNATE enough during the year 1978 to enjoy two holiday trips, the first to Nepal. I won a free round-trip ticket offered by Royal Nepal Airlines as a lottery prize at an FCCT social occasion.

The short flight to Kathmandu was the first non-working trip I made beyond Thailand's borders and its neighboring Indochina countries suffering from Communist takeovers. (I traveled to Hong Kong the previous year to coordinate coverage in Thailand for the German television network NDR-ARD, who hired me to help them gain access to refugee camps in Thailand.)

The visit to Nepal lasted a week. Besides sightseeing trips around the capital, I enjoyed the short flight along the Himalayas range to view Mount Everest. I spent the last night in the lovely provincial capital of Pokhara before boarding a long-distance bus the next morning to travel to India. I wanted to visit Varanasi, or Benares, at the bend in the River Ganges, famous for its sacred waters where thousands of Hindus celebrate funeral rites.

Pokhara is nestled just below the Annapurna Mountains. I was enchanted with the natural beauty of the entire area, the picturesque Phewa Lake, and gorgeous bougainvilleas and Royal Poinciana trees along many downtown streets.

I left Pokhara on an intercity bus to the border and transferred to an Indian bus to take me to the railhead at Gorakhpur. In Gorakhpur I had my first exposure in the Subcontinent to the enormous numbers of people of all ages and both sexes escaping the evening heat by trying to sleep in the immense plaza in front of the train station.

My train ride to Varanasi arrived in the middle of the night. I wanted to visit Varanasi to see how the Hindu holiday (similar to its Thai cousin) of *Songkran* was celebrated. In Thailand, the several days of *Songkran* festivities welcome in the Thai New Year by "cleansing" others in ceremonial water showers: water is thrown with abandon on friends, relatives, and strangers, to wash away the metaphoric sins and unpleasant events of the previous year.

I quickly learned one major difference of Songkran between Thailand and India. In India, the water is spiked with food coloring; in Thailand, plain uncolored water is used. I had an open-air cyclo driver take me to the vicinity around the river where Hindus gathered for funeral rites. By the time the driver had reached that area, I was soaked with numerous instantaneous baths and with clothes covered with mixes of colors.

I quickly changed my mind and asked to be taken back to the hotel. From there I made a quick change of clothes and took a taxi to the airport, where I flew to Kathmandu and boarded my return flight to Bangkok. I had learned all I wanted to know about the differences in celebrating Songkran between India and Thailand!

The second leisure trip that year lasted slightly more than a month: my first exposure to Europe. I purchased a complicated routing to take me to Frankfurt, London, Hamburg, Munich, Paris, and New York. I transited Frankfurt immediately for the short flight to London to visit the BBC and meet editors who handled my reporting from Bangkok over the last several months.

I quickly learned first hand about the tiny economy hotel rooms in London: hardly any floor space aside from a small shower stall, a single bed, and a small desk and chair. One actor in the 1983 American movie *Flashdance* joked about such a room, "You had to leave it to change your mind."

I spent one evening on a London pub crawl with George Lewinski, the bureau chief in London for the Canadian Broadcasting Corporation (CBC). He was paying me for occasional radio reports for their *CBC Sunday Morning* magazine, a summary of that week's major global stories.

I flew next to Hamburg, Germany to spend a few days with German cameraman Henning Huge and his family. His ARD-NDR network was paying me as a field producer in Thailand to act as an interpreter and help gather video images in many refugee camps. His family showered me with authentic German *gemütlichkeit,* so much so that I postponed my stop in Munich until my return from the US.

The lasting observation I had from West Germany was the stark new condition of private automobiles, presumably throughout the entire country. The great majority of automobiles on the roads in Bangkok were much older—especially non-air-conditioned, ubiquitous Datsun Blue Bird taxis. Automobile air-conditioning would become more and more standard in the coming years in taxis and also in city buses, but not back then. Wealthy Thai residents drove late-model Mercedes, BMWs, Volvos, Jaguars, and other high-priced European sedans. Those numbers were scarce compared to inexpensive Japanese (and Italian—mostly Fiat) vehicles, and hardly any American-made automobiles.

From Hamburg I flew to the US to see my parents and sisters and attend the ten-year reunion of my 1968 class at West Point. The return flight to Bangkok took me back through Frankfurt. I boarded the *Deutshe Bahn* to Munich to spend a few days.

Since it was still early summer, construction of the huge *Oktoberfest* beer tents and assorted buildings had not yet begun. On my only Saturday morning, I took the suburban S-Bahn train that disembarked near the Andechs Monastery and Brewery. My intent was for sightseeing and sampling of its world-famous beer. From Andechs, I launched my solo *volksmarch* along Bavarian byways to the famous Lake Starnberg and the resort town by the same name. As I walked along the well-maintained roads, the rolling hills reminded me of long stretches of farmland in Iowa and its Heartland neighbors. The next day I rode back to Frankfurt and boarded the long flight back to Thailand.

# # #

CHAPTER 8

A Strange Visit to Angkor Wat; Diplomats Flee Cambodia, December 1978–February 1979

I LANDED IN Bangkok just as the Indochina refugee crisis was worsening dramatically. The refugees, almost all of whom were penniless, began showing up in numerous border provinces in Thailand, telling their own individual stories about their decisions to seek freedom from Communist persecution, especially in Cambodia under the radical Communist Khmer Rouge regime led by Pol Pot and his inner circle, the Gang of Six (i.e., he and Ieng Sary and both their wives plus Khieu Samphan and Son Sen).

Khieu Samphan, inside northern Cambodia, 1980.

Our news crew traveled frequently over the next few years to interview refugees in camps in several locations: Nong Khai in the northeast, where the majority of Laotian refugees were housed; Surin in the northeast to Aranyapratet in the east housing Cambodian refugees; and Chantaburi in the southeast and Songkhla in the far south, for Vietnamese boat people refugees.

The Laotian refugees were primarily ethnic Hmong hill tribes. Most adult men had served alongside mercenaries from Thailand and American CIA advisors during the "secret war" in Laos. More information follows on the changing conditions with Cambodian and Vietnamese refugees and boat people.

Hatcher with working conditions, 1978–1980.

The refugees told sad personal stories of extreme hardship, suffering, and loss, including stories of others dying during the escape. Propagandists for the new Communist regimes, including American sympathizers, dismissed many of the refugees' stories as being greatly embellished or fabricated to embarrass the new Communist rulers in Saigon, renamed Ho Chi Minh City, and in Phnom Penh and Vientiane. I would be fortunate enough to visit all three capitals, along with other locations inside all three countries, as the regimes gradually relaxed restrictions on visits by journalists.

Among the most memorable stories was a daylong visit to the twelfth-century Angkor Wat temple complex in northwest Cambodia. That visit came about from an agreement between the Phnom Penh regime and a senior Thai government official, in hopes of starting one-day tours from Bangkok to visit Angkor Wat.

In December 1978 I was recalled from a news trip to New Delhi to travel to Cambodia on the maiden flight. A handful of journalists and one or two American businesspeople were allowed on the aircraft. Because of a mix-up in names while I was in New Delhi, I was listed as the CBS News representative rather than our staff cameraman Kurt Hoefle. I was not a professional cameraman and had no experience at all in shooting film on the Auricon 16mm news camera. The Auricon was the camera of choice by overseas crews, just before the American networks converted to videotape cameras and equipment. Luckily for me, Kurt was able to give me a rushed tutorial on operating the Auricon camera. My competition was with Neil Davis of NBC News and Klaes Bratt of ABC News, both professional cameramen. Neil Davis's biggest claim to fame during the Vietnam War was his filming on the grounds of the Presidential Palace in Saigon as the North Vietnamese Army tanks broke through the fences and gates surrounding the palace grounds to seize power from the failing South Vietnamese government. Neil and Klaes were close friends, albeit competitors.

Once our morning flight landed at the nearby Siem Reap airport close to Angkor Wat, we were placed in an airport VIP room.

Under house arrest 1978, Siem Reap airport, Cambodia:
L-Jim Rooney, American businessman; R-David
DeVoss, *Time* magazine Bangkok bureau chief.

It became obvious that the delay was longer than necessary. The three American cameramen had times booked on satellites for our stories upon return to Bangkok. The same Thai government official succeeded in getting approval from Cambodian leadership at the airport for all of us to board buses for the short trip to Angkor Wat.

We were allowed to record film footage of much of the temple complex but without any in-depth information briefings or any assigned foreign ministry or other staff from the new regime. Only the most basic history of the complex itself. To my knowledge no civilians were allowed to visit the hallowed complex.

The ambiance of the countryside was surreal. On our way back to the airport, we were able to get off the bus briefly and take supplemental film footage of small knots of Cambodian farmers. There was no opportunity to interview any of the farmers. We reasoned that all of them had probably been instructed not to acknowledge us in any way. Nonetheless, we were able to gather footage of farmers on farmland and rice paddies near the road.

Upon arrival in Bangkok, the three of us cameramen transferred to the evening flight to Hong Kong, where employees at film labs would process our film. We each wrote our individual stories, to be approved in New York before we recorded our narrations.

I was unprepared to travel to Hong Kong. I had to relay a message to our Bangkok driver to go to my rented bungalow and pack a couple changes of clothes and a minimum of toiletries. He did not know what to pack and did not have much time. I remember having to manage wearing the same clothing the next day before getting time to buy a few extra items.

Staying for one or two days for any follow-up of the story that CBS may have wanted, I shopped for some clothes but mostly enjoyed experiencing the first five-star hotel in my life, the Mandarin Hotel in Central District: such a plush room in such a luxury hotel!

While in Hong Kong, I became aware of the other story making worldwide news—coming out of Phnom Penh. Two American newspaper reporters, Elizabeth Becker of the *Washington Post* and Richard Dudman of the *St. Louis Post-Dispatch*, had received visas issued by the Pol Pot regime to report on the situation in Cambodia. Among their reporting of first-person accounts around the capital, and interviews with top Khmer Rouge leaders, both reported being panic-stricken one evening when unidentified saboteurs attacked their government guesthouse they were in at the time.

No one group took responsibility for the strange attack. Both Becker and Dudman survived the scare. Rumors quickly circulated throughout Asia that the attackers may have been North Vietnamese sappers; or false flag operatives of the Khmer Rouge; or petty criminals stealing valuables of either of the Americans.

The other non-journalism aspect of the short stay in Hong Kong came via a local vendor selling magazines from his sidewalk stall next to the Mandarin Hotel. One of the headlines on the cover of that month's issue of *Playboy* caught my attention: "Europe, a Motorcycle, and You." I had done some leisure riding in Arizona during my time at Fort Huachuca, and rented a small motorcycle once or twice in Thailand to explore the countryside outside Pattaya Beach.

I was intrigued by the title. I bought the magazine and quickly skimmed the article, which named two tour operators who ran tours of the Alps. I loved the story and wrote one of the tour operators, Michael Von Thielmann, a German-born naturalized American living in San Diego, asking for more information on that year's tour in early September. Each year's tour ended back in Munich on the first day of *Oktoberfest*. Each tour rode several days to reach a major Mediterranean tourist mecca anywhere from Spain to Yugoslavia, and returned to Munich via different routing.

Brochure of Alpine motorcycle tours, 1983.

Michael gave riders the opportunity to purchase a new BMW motorcycle directly off the assembly line in Munich. Riders had the option to rent motorcycles for mountain riding, or air-conditioned cars to enjoy the same routes. I put a deposit down on the newest motorcycle that BMW had begun to manufacture, the R65, a 650-cc model. I observed once on the roads that the R65 was the perfect size for mountain riding. Although its engine was smaller than more powerful, larger motorcycles, the R65 had the greater maneuverability in the hairpin turns in the mountains. The extremely high cost of gasoline in Europe was offset by the mileage of most motorcycles; the R65 achieved between fifty or fifty-five miles per gallon.

The reader will find my tour report from that first Von Thielmann tour later.

I returned to Bangkok to continue my daily reporting on major international stories involving refugees and cross-border incidents across all four neighboring countries. I also was available to cover stories taking me to Singapore and Malaysia when given assignments there.

Just as the new year began, Cambodia's national radio station began urgently broadcasting that the North Vietnamese Army was attacking Phnom Penh. The attacks forced the evacuation to Thailand of diplomats from countries accredited to the Khmer Rouge regime, universally from the PRC and pro-Chinese Communist countries.

Many of us realized the irony. The evacuation mimicked an overland convoy three and half years earlier, when diplomats and other expatriates abandoned Phnom Penh hurriedly after the seizure of power by the Khmer Rouge.

The destination for both evacuations was the same: the Thai district capital of Aranyapratet and same border town that served as a center for humanitarian volunteers aiding Cambodian refugees before and during 1979.

There was a small stream separating Aranyapratet from its sister town, Poipet, on the Cambodian side. Diplomats crossed into Thailand at the barely sufficient gate overseen by immigration officers on both sides.

By the time our CBS crew reached the area, the evacuees had been cordoned off in a large, empty field a short distance from the actual border. There were diplomats from different countries, along with other Asians who seemed to be Chinese or North Korean mercenaries acting as paramilitary advisors to the Khmer Rouge. The suspected Chinese mercenaries also seemed to be carrying large duffel bags and were refusing any efforts by the Thai authorities to conduct any searches of the bags, thought to contain various military articles including possible small arms and assorted ammunition. Such a possibility gave confirmation to earlier information from intelligence sources in Bangkok that the PRC had sent numerous advisors to provide military resources to the Khmer Rouge.

The Bangkok-based embassy staff from affected countries were taking responsibility for their charges among the numerous arrivals. Within a day or two, the three English-language wire services—AP, UPI, and Reuters—began reporting that a semisecret helicopter airlift by Royal Thai Army aviation crews had reportedly flown the top Khmer Rouge leaders out of

Cambodia and transferred them to China aboard fixed-wing aircraft of unknown registration. No confirmation was ever forthcoming. The situation was so fluid that most reporters dropped the rumors.

# # #

CHAPTER 9

Open Warfare Breaks Out Along the China-Vietnam Border, February–March 1979

IN FEBRUARY, RADIO broadcasts from Radio Hanoi began mentioning a major Chinese Peoples' Liberation Army attack to destroy Vietnam's border defenses and to demonstrate China's strong objection to Hanoi's takeover of Cambodia the previous year. In another supreme irony, logistics support for Vietnam for internal defense and for the military occupation of Cambodia came from the Soviet Union. Both major Communist powers were locked in a proxy war in Southeast Asia.

BBC editors in London called me the first day of radio broadcasts to ask me to file reports throughout the day from knowledgeable sources in Bangkok.

I soon learned that the foreign editor for CBS News, Brian Ellis, had agreed months earlier to an unusual request from the US Congress. Brian had been promoted to foreign editor after a distinguished time as Asia bureau chief in Hong Kong. Two members of the House of Representatives, Democrat Elizabeth Holtzman of New York and Republican Billy Lee Evans of Georgia, planned to travel to Hanoi in early 1979 to discuss the issue of American POWs who might still be alive and held captive in North Vietnam (or possibly under North Vietnamese control in Laos). The Congressional staffers planning the trip had asked Mr. Ellis if CBS would consider accompanying the two members of Congress if the trip did occur.

Brian Ellis, CBS News foreign editor, New York, 1982.

Brian had been the Saigon bureau chief for CBS before the end of the Vietnam War. During the last several weeks of the war, he had coura-geously begun exfiltrating from the country a large number of reporters and families from a number of news agencies besides CBS. He and others, especially American diplomat and refugee coordinator Lionel Rosenblatt, were instrumental in organizing such a laudable effort. Those so fortunate to escape were spared the great uncertainty and agony of whatever punish-ment, incarceration, and even "re-education" that the North Vietnamese political commissars might enact when assuming power.

Brian advised our crew that the trip seemed to be on and that three of us in the Bangkok bureau were to submit visa applications to the Viet-namese embassy. CBS soundman Derek Williams was out of the country on personal leave. The three of us acquiring visas were reporter Peter Collins, cameraman Kurt Hoefle, and me. One other Western journalist, Alan Daw-son of UPI in Bangkok, was also given a visa.

On a hot and humid Bangkok morning, we four news representatives and Ms. Holtzman and Mr. Evans, with key subordinates, departed on

Air Vietnam to Hanoi, arriving in the middle of the afternoon at Gia Lam airport, where we observed a row of Soviet-made MIG-21s on the tarmac or in revetments along the taxiway. Almost immediately after we were in the passenger vehicles en route to our government guesthouse, one of our Foreign Ministry escorts said that the Foreign Ministry was sponsoring a trip to the Chinese border the next day to view the hostilities, and would our small group be interested in joining the trip! We could not answer quickly enough in the affirmative.

That evening we attended a press conference where Foreign Minister Nguyen Co Thach gave his government's official position on that day's combat developments. Sometime later, Thach would become famous for his witty comment about the Communist regime in Hanoi: "We are not without accomplishment. We have managed to distribute poverty equally!"

Early the next morning, the four of us boarded two Soviet-made jeeps (Collins and Dawson in one jeep, Hoefle and I in the other) and joined the caravan of Hanoi-based journalists, all of whom were from Warsaw Pact allies—including Poland, Bulgaria, and East Germany, inter alia. I had no way to know if any Russians were on the trip. Our overnight stop en route was the military barracks at Yen Bai, where we spent the evening, ate a simple dinner, and enjoyed excellent Polish beer that the Polish reporter had brought along.

The next morning our caravan reached the outskirts of Lao Cai on the border. We were close enough to hear the explosions and feel the vibrations from several rounds of incoming Chinese artillery. One such barrage lasted for three or four minutes of nonstop artillery fire. We were not close enough to the intended targets of the barrages, but we did encounter large numbers of Vietnamese civilians escaping their houses in the tiny farming villages. All the civilians, primarily women and children, were on foot, except for fording streams in the area. They were carrying all their worldly goods. No vehicles were among the sad pedestrian convoy escaping from the border.

Our foreign ministry escorts had two tasks: to safeguard all of us (especially Congressman Evans) and, for classified reasons, to prevent any of us nosy Western journalists from getting any closer to the border. We could not deviate from what the escorts wanted. Our handlers and host military officers at the front brought out a handful of supposed Chinese soldiers for us to view. Some bore bruised faces and other marks of physical beating. Our escorts said the prisoners had been captured sometime earlier.

Captured PLA soldiers.

Congresswoman Holtzman had gone with the second caravan with other Hanoi-based journalists to a second border crossing at Lang Son. We had no idea how their journey transpired or what they were able to observe around Lang Son.

Because the escorts wanted to get all our group back to Hanoi later that evening, the caravan turned around just after noontime and began heading back to the capital.

As we departed the border, we came upon a stopped jeep. A foreign news crew (who turned out to be Bulgarian) was filming a sleepy and peaceful village of thatched-roof huts close to the artillery barrage. All of a sudden, the cameraman saw in his viewfinder an artillery round landing right in the middle of the village and setting several huts on fire.

Border village on fire from Chinese artillery.

Our jeep came to a right-angle turn in the road. We told the driver to stop. Kurt and I both jumped out. While Kurt filmed the inferno, I snapped several color photographs showing villages with flames engulfing the roofs and walls. I would be very lucky, as I explain later, to be paid handsomely by *Newsweek* for its cover photo the following week on the international edition, with global distribution.

Vietnamese civilians fleeing artillery.

Vietnamese civilians fleeing artillery.

Vietnamese civilians fleeing artillery and fighting.

Our caravan reached Hanoi close to midnight after brief stops for fuel and restroom breaks. The overriding impression all the way back was the fairly high heat coming up from the heavy steel floorboards, maybe added to the jeep to protect occupants from antipersonnel mines. Kurt and I could rest our feet on the floor for only a few seconds at a time. We joked all the way back to speed the time and to convince ourselves that this hot ordeal was one small occupational hazard in the middle of such an explosive (pardon the pun) story.

We departed Hanoi early the next morning, a Saturday. Sixty hours from our arrival, we were back at Gia Lam Airport. We observed a large IL-76 Ilyushin cargo aircraft apparently offloading Soviet arms and military supplies.

Soviet cargo aircraft.

We boarded our flight on Royal Air Lao, that country's national airline. Laos would formally become the Lao Peoples' Democratic Republic later in 1979, backed by the North Vietnamese Army and political leadership from Hanoi.

The late Vietnamese dictator Ho Chi Minh had envisioned a unified Indochina with South Vietnam, Cambodia, and Laos under North Vietnam's control. The ongoing struggles in both other countries after 1975 seemed to fulfill his dream.

We landed in the Laotian capital of Vientiane to change planes for Bangkok. A very pleasant surprise awaited us. The four of us journalists were met by American embassy staff saying that the US embassy in Bangkok had sent its US Air Force C-12 passenger aircraft (a variation of the King 200 civilian aircraft) to carry us back. The comparable luxury flight was a very pleasing end to our whirlwind trip to the Sino-Vietnamese border war (and from having to endure the heat from the steel floorboards in our Vietnamese jeeps the day before).

We managed to process all the film in Bangkok for satellite transmission later that evening to New York for broadcast on the Saturday evening news and for rebroadcast on Sunday.

One of the idiosyncrasies occurred as a result of the timing of the first CBS News television broadcast to US audiences that Saturday night. Earlier than that broadcast, however, was a television report by the BBC. They had legal permission to download the CBS satellite footage and transmit it to its customers worldwide.

The small kerfuffel was that I had filed one or two radio stories to the BBC that Saturday afternoon from our office. When the BBC editors in London received my radio stories, they married my reporting up with the CBS film footage and aired all as a film report and credited me as working for the BBC.

That worldwide BBC television story was broadcast hours before the Saturday night New York time broadcast of the CBS television story narrated by Peter Collins. Understandably there were ruffled feathers in New York over my using CBS resources to report for the BBC—before CBS had the chance to air such a dramatic story.

Brian Ellis tactfully advised me of my mistake. I had not realized that any narration I would be sending to BBC might complicate matters. I easily understood, however, the technical ethical misuse of CBS resources to report for the BBC.

One of the fellows who walked into our Bangkok office that Saturday afternoon was an American who claimed to represent a small photo agency in New York, and asked if we wanted to sell any photographs. Kurt and I agreed for the agency *Photoreporters,* and its owner Ernie Boehm, to represent us and pay us royalties for all worldwide use, with *Newsweek* having the right of first refusal.

The use by *Newsweek* of my photo on its international cover that following week, and my first-person story inside the magazine contributed to a very lucrative sixty hours in North Vietnam for me, and for Kurt. We shared fees we earned from the photographs. I also was fortunate to earn fees from my BBC radio reports and my separate radio reports for CBS.

My cordial and easy relationship with *Photoreporters* would last for the next few years whenever Mr. Boehm marketed my photographs from various ongoing geopolitical events in the region. He was able to move many of my photographs I provided from the Philippines to India and Pakistan whenever on assignment for either of the two broadcast news agencies or *Newsweek.*

#   #   #

CHAPTER 10

An Unusual Return of Used American Warplanes from Southeast Asia, April 1979

IN EARLY APRIL 1979, my former military boss in USMACTHAI was running his business in retirement importing Thai wicker and rattan furniture and household furnishings to Thailand to sell in his retail store in Fort Walton Beach, Florida, close to Eglin Air Force Base and Hurlburt Field. The latter facility was home to the air force special operations forces. That former boss, twice-retired Air Force Brigadier General Harry C. "Heinie" Aderholt was a legend in the Florida Panhandle and around the world for his flying heroics in secret missions in World War II and the Korean War. Those missions were first under the auspices of the US Army Air Corps and later the US Air Force. He also flew secret missions for the Central Intelligence Agency in the early 1950s. In the mid-1960s he commanded the 56th Air Commando Wing (Special Operations Wing) based in northeast Thailand, very close to the Mekong River.

That unit operated large helicopters to rescue downed American pilots in North Vietnam and Laos. As commander, he also coordinated close air support missions for Laotian freedom fighters and Thai mercenaries inside

Laos. He retired from that assignment as a full colonel but was recalled to active duty to command the joint units in Bangkok to which I would be assigned. The Defense Department apparently wanted him back in Southeast Asia for his long-standing relationships with the highest levels of the Royal Thai Armed Forces. He was my most senior rating officer from 1973 to 1974. His command then also extended to advisory units at several bases around the country.

Heinie asked me during one of his buying trips if CBS News would be interested in a very strange legacy story from that special operations wing close to the Mekong River. Heinie said that the US Air Force attempted to evacuate large amounts of American military equipment from South Vietnam. Heinie had managed to appropriate, without Washington's knowledge, four US Air Force A-1 Skyraider airplanes.

The A-1 Skyraider was a single-engine propeller aircraft used extensively not only in South Vietnam but also by American pilots making bombing runs in Laos against the Communist Pathet Lao and their North Vietnamese advisors. South Vietnamese pilots had managed to fly a total of twenty-nine A-1s to Thailand in 1975. The US General Services Administration had impounded twenty-five of the A-1s, thinking that was the correct number. Heinie had managed to have loyal pilots conceal the remaining four A-1s at Takhli Air Base under control of the Thai base commander—a good friend of Heinie's.

Transfer of USAF A-1 Skyraiders from Thailand to USA.

Loading A-1 Skyraider into river barge.

Heinie told me that he had promised to deliver the four A-1s to a non-profit flying museum in the US, called *Yesterday's Air Force*. I had no idea of any financial arrangements he made with anyone.

Adding: Postscript: With all the demands of our news efforts in that climactic year, the eventual fate of the four airplanes remains shrouded in mystery. No one knows what happened after the shipment of the aircraft to the US. Brigadier General Heinie Aderholt passed away in 2010 in Fort Walton Beach, FL. I was fortunate to attend his funeral and rub shoulders with true American heroes like Medal of Honor winner Bud Day (since deceased) and Lawrence "Larry" Ropka, inter alia.

What Heinie managed to do, as our CBS television story would show, was to tow the A-1s behind heavy-duty pickup trucks with jerry-built tow bars. The unusual transport was from Takhli along a busy highway to a small river port for loading onto specially modified river barges.

Even with the wings folded over the fuselage, the shortened wingspan of each aircraft was still too wide to allow the aircraft to be lowered upright into each barge. So, Heinie had paid for Thai welders to cut out sections on the barges' steel sides to allow for the aircraft to sit comfortably for the river voyage to the Bangkok's major port of Klong Toei. Ocean-going cargo vessels would complete the long voyage to the USA.

Retired air force general Heinie Aderholt flipping a breakfast omelet.

So, on that Sunday afternoon and evening, my cameraman Narong, our driver, and I joined the unusual procession down the highway to the riverport. Narong gathered video images of nearly all aspects, including the operation of heavy-duty cranes to lift each aircraft onto one of the barges. We returned to Bangkok.

My narration hopefully befitted the whole escapade and the history of the A-1 as a close air-support aircraft in South Vietnam and Laos. We shipped the film and narration off to New York. Such a colorful story was made for television and was broadcast on the morning news later that week. I never secured a copy of the story, regrettably. I regarded it as another great short documentary on some lesser-known aspects of the entire American involvement in Indochina.

The news load of reporting on overlapping political and sociological stories in all three neighboring countries allowed some quasi-normality for the next few months. I was able to fly to the US to see my parents in Iowa and both sisters—Carole in the Denver area and Cathy in the Twin Cities. Carole had remarried the previous year. I was able to get to know my new brother-in-law, Roger Royther, during my days in Denver.

As I began my return to Bangkok, two events temporarily interceded. American Airlines flight 191 flying between Chicago O'Hare and Los Angeles crashed on May 25, killing all 271 persons on board and two on the ground. All commercial airlines had their DC-10 fleets grounded while investigations began looking into the cause, later determined to be "improper maintenance."

When I reached San Francisco en route to Asia, airlines normally flying the DC-10 on those routes were having to reroute passengers onto other wide-body aircraft like the Boeing 747 or the Lockheed L-1011.

My return to Bangkok was delayed. While I was waiting for new reservations, an ABC reporter named Bill Stewart was murdered by National Guard forces in Nicaragua. He was reporting on the revolution there led by the Sandanistas. CBS News among other news agencies reduced their presence in Managua. Foreign editor Brian Ellis asked if I wanted to volunteer to go to Nicaragua. I had no interest at the time in Central America and did not speak Spanish, so I gracefully declined.

#   #   #

CHAPTER 11

Operation Seasweep—
The Dramatic Rescue of
Vietnamese Boat People, 1979

I MANAGED TO get back to Bangkok without much delay. I immediately became aware of another story opportunity, this time in Singapore. With more and more refugees escaping from South Vietnam, the famous "boat people" at the time, many charitable organizations were engaged in major relief efforts in many places—Thailand, the Philippines, Malaysia, Indonesia, and Hong Kong.

Our CBS representative in Singapore had alerted New York to the American nonprofit organization *WorldVision*, which was chartering an aging cargo vessel to patrol the South China Sea. Its purpose was to assist any boat people as they made the dangerous trip to freedom in a continuing hodge-podge of small fishing boats, mostly along a thin channel of water called Refugee Alley. It extended from the tip of South Vietnam to the long shoreline of Thailand and nearby Malaysian islands.

I was dispatched to Singapore to join a Hong Kong–based freelance film cameraman and a longtime CBS employee in our bureau there, Michael Lam. We gained permission to accompany the *WorldVision* staff and the ship's crew on one or more relief missions in the South China Sea.

Once at sea, in the aging cargo vessel that *WorldVision* had renamed *Sea Sweep*, we settled on a slow heading up Refugee Alley. Within a few days, we came upon a tiny fishing boat floating helplessly with white flags flying. Crammed on board: ninety-three Vietnamese men, women, and children.

We pulled alongside and took the captain of the small fishing boat on board. The engineer on *Sea Sweep* went on board the fishing boat and determined that the motor was beyond repair.

The original mission of *Sea Sweep* was to provide relief to any refugees but do nothing to rescue them. Rather, to allow them to continue their journey. The *WorldVision* staff did not want to be accused by the respective governments of trying to offload refugees anywhere.

But once *WorldVision* president Stanley Mooneyham, who was on board, understood that the fishing boat was no longer seaworthy, the decision was made to take all the refugees on board whatever the international consequences.

Sea Sweep swept the sea and saved those boat people.

Once on board, the refugees began to describe their treacherous ordeal at sea. Fortunately, none of the refugees needed any major medical attention. Those with minor issues responded quickly to treatment from *WorldVision* medical staff.

The refugees left southern South Vietnam a month earlier. Speculation for years was that large numbers of boat people perished at sea, but no refugee statistics included such deaths. This group said they sailed for several days before encountering Thai pirates, who viciously boarded the boat, robbed the refugees of their valuables, and raped many of the women.

The boat eventually landed in Malaysia. The refugees were quickly placed in an outdoor corral with no shelter from the elements. After a few days, they were told that the authorities would not allow them to stay in Malaysia.

The refugees were forced back onto their boat, then towed at high speed for twenty-four hours into international waters, where their towline was cut. For the next several days, with an inoperable motor, the fishing boat resembled a floating coffin. Refugees claimed that more than one huge oceangoing cargo vessel ignored them.

When *Sea Sweep* showed up, it was a miracle. I ended my story on *CBS Evening News* once we returned to Singapore, saying, "These ninety-three Vietnamese refugees, found floating hopelessly in the South China Sea, characterize the tens of thousands of boat people and other refugees from Indochina, all desperately seeking a better future, but by no means certain of finding it."

There was another curve to our landing in Singapore. *Sea Sweep* had smuggled all ninety-three refugees into a small refugee camp without the knowledge of the Singaporean authorities. By the time the next morning rolled around, our story had run on CBS. By network news standards, it was fairly long for the evening news. It timed out at two minutes and forty-five seconds. Any story over one to one and a half minutes was a long story.

Authorities in Singapore had become aware of the smuggling effort. No one in our crew knew anything. I was summoned that Saturday morning to the Foreign Ministry and told that technically, *Sea Sweep*'s return to Singapore without official entry permission was illegal. I was warned of the possible punishments. However, the authorities realized that any penalty against any one of the crew, and certainly against a reporter from a major American news network, would backfire from the negative publicity on the heels of a poignant refugee story. I was told in so many words, "Don't let it happen again."

The short stays in Singapore before and after *Sea Sweep*'s "sweeping the sea" allowed me to cross off a "bucket list" item, long before bucket lists became cool. I was able to visit the iconic Raffles Hotel and its equally iconic Long Bar. On one or two occasions, I enjoyed one of the Lion City's most famous creations, an authentic Singapore Sling, at the site of its first creation. Tout de suite.

# # #

CHAPTER 12

From Singapore to Motorcycles in the Alps, July–September 1979

THE NEXT FEW weeks back in Bangkok were uneventful. The continuing stream of events throughout the region created plenty of work, with information flowing largely from diplomatic sources and military attachés, and from sources within the Thai military and international refugee organizations.

I spent time during the first part of August planning and preparing for my three-week holiday in Europe, when I would join others on the Alpine motorcycle tour. The tour leader, Michael von Thielmann, advised me that my order for a new BMW motorcycle had been confirmed. Mine was not the only new BMW motorcycle that riders in the group had ordered.

I flew to Amsterdam on KLM Airlines and the next morning enjoyed a delightful morning jog in a large and manicured public park before heading back to the airport for the short flight to Munich. I was becoming somewhat of a world traveler, albeit a very small-time one, over the last several months. I counted two transoceanic trips, the first one being to Europe and across the Atlantic to the US. The second trip was across the Pacific to the US. I had made several regional flights around Southeast Asia or domestic flights inside Thailand.

At Schiphol Airport I was able to rendezvous with Michael and several American and Canadian riders. We spent the next two days in Munich picking up our motorcycles from the BMW factory and shopping for new helmets and motorcycle clothing.

Michael had honed his tours for maximum comfort, freedom, and camaraderie for all riders, regardless of one's motorcycle skills, with easily reachable day by day destinations. All riders could leave their main luggage in the hotel lobby each morning and have it hauled to the next hotel, where it would be waiting for the riders. Michael drove his own van and was able to carry anyone who did not wish to ride a motorcycle. A very capable BMW motorcycle mechanic accompanied the tour in another van, to help any rider with any mechanical or other problems along the way. Luggage was easily carried in both vans.

Each day's itinerary allowed maximum freedom of choice for the riders. Each rider could travel in a group, by him- or herself, or divide up the day as preferred. Michael printed out several possible points of interest on each day's general route. The decision to visit any point of interest was up to each rider.

Continental breakfasts every morning were included in the tour price. Approximately half of the other meals, especially evening meals, also were included in the tour price.

Because I was a bachelor, I was assigned a male roommate for the tour: Joergen, an ethnic German who had emigrated to the US and lived in Lake Tahoe. He was a veteran mountain rider and helpful when we traveled together.

I was fortunate to escape any injury or damage on the tour. I suffered only one fall. One late afternoon in France, I rounded a slight uphill turn with loose gravel on the shoulder. I did not accelerate fast enough coming out of the turn and the tires hit the loose gravel. The bike went over on one side, but I was able to right the motorcycle quickly and rode on without any damage or injury.

The publicized destination of that year's tour was the Spanish resort town of Sitges south of Barcelona. Little did I realize it at the time, but I was already automatically a member of the Alpine motorcycle fraternity of men and women. And not only in the Alps but virtually anywhere in the world, where motorcyclists pass each other on the roads large and small and exchange knowing waves to affirm that fraternity.

From our comfortable hotel in Puchheim outside Munich, we rode southwest and crossed Lake Konstanz into Switerzerland. One of the highlights of those first few days was the short stop in Lucerne, where I enjoyed my walk across the famous covered Kapelbrucke (Chapel Bridge) built in 1333. The readers should understand that each day's rides may or may not have included others.

We continued through Interlaken and other Alpine towns and onto the north shore of Lake Leman near the town of Lausanne. I took personal satisfaction riding through Lausanne. From my years in Thailand, I remembered that the king at the time, King Bhumibhol, before assuming the monarchy in 1950, had lived in the Canton of Vaud for seventeen years and attended the University of Lausanne. The same King Bhumibhol (1927–2016) was far more revered in life than his son and present king—who maintains luxury lodgings outside Munich during his frequent visits to temporarily slough off his regal duties in Thailand.

After Lausanne and Lake Leman, we traveled through the scenic Rhône River valley. We stopped briefly in Avignon to visit the Palace of the Popes—a lovely Gothic granite structure that took seventy years to build (1252–1322) as a temporary papal residence and focus of Western Christianity during the fourteenth century. Today it is a UNESCO World Heritage Site.

This first half of the trip, heading to Barcelona and Sitges, skirted the higher Alpine reaches and "robbed me" of experiences in the following years of Alpine riding: swerving along the dozens of mountain in Bavaria, Austria, Switzerland, northern Croatia, and northern Italy. In future years,

I was fortunate to traverse famous mountain passes, and ride up and down other mountain roads throughout the Alps. The three most famous mountain passes I traversed were the Zugspitze in Bavaria on the west, Stelvio between Austria and Italy to the east, and further east, the Austrian pass at Grossglockner. More on this most enjoyable aspect in later chapters.

The forty-eight-hour respite along the Mediterranean in Sitges was relaxing in the generally laid back ambiance from Spain to the former Yugoslavia (our tour destination in three of the next four years). From Sitges we journeyed back through southern France, with a memorable stopover in Carcassone, a city and fortress since the fifth century occupied by the Romans until the demise of the Western Roman Empire.

Joergen and I rode together along the French coast to another forty-eight-hour stopover in Toulon near Marseille. We lounged in complete sunshine the second day on Ile du Levant, Levant Island. Ten percent of land on the island is a nudist resort Heliopolis founded in 1932. The reader may have a hard time deciding whether or not I hid behind bushes most of the afternoon, mimicking Peter Sellers in the classic motion picture *A Shot in the Dark.*

I remember stopping in the town of Montpelier one afternoon to get basic directions to our Novotel hotel on the outskirts. I walked into a downtown bar in the midafternoon. There were no customers as I recall. I asked the bartender in my best French, "Ou est l'hotel Novotel?" He motioned with hands and arms and mumbled something. I nodded without understanding and walked out to my motorcycle. As I balanced the handlebars to lift the kickstand, I glanced down the sidewalk to see a *belle jeune fille* (beautiful young lady) walking towards me. She was wearing a stunning faux-leather pink pantsuit. I desperately searched my brain to think of something witty to say in French.

As I started to lift my right leg over the motorcycle, disaster struck. A brief rain shower earlier that afternoon had created a mixture at the curb of standing water, leaked engine oil, and mud and gravel. The rubber tires began to slide sideways in that wet mess. I lost my balance, fell headfirst across the bike, and landed awkwardly on the sidewalk.

Somehow, the lady disappeared. To this day I don't know whether she quickly walked past me or turned around and retraced her steps, wanting nothing to do with this born loser! I did manage to find the Novotel by heading out in the general direction the bartender had indicated and watching for highway signs advertising the hotel.

From Toulon, Joergen and I rode together, stopping once or twice to enjoy ripening grapes in vineyards. We bypassed all the famous cities of the French Riviera including Monaco, before heading north to Turin, Italy. From Turin I rode alone and headed east toward our overnight stay in Riva del Garda. That solo ride taught me a cardinal rule about when not to ride if possible: in a major rainstorm, on the high-speed Autostradas in Italy or the Autobahns in Germany.

For a few hours that miserable afternoon, I endured wet misery rather than cower under any overpasses (which were rare, as I remember). Instead, I pushed on in the slowest lane, being passed by nonstop traffic from heavy trucks and other vehicles, all drenching me in waves of water. Even with my rain gear, I was completely drenched. The visor on my inexpensive helmet did not work well in the mix of rain and high humidity. It would fog up within seconds of my lowering it to shed the falling rain. But in raising the visor, I opened up my entire face to the walls of water from the passing vehicles and the steady fall of pelting rain. Up and down, up and down with the visor, with no dry solution at hand.

But knowing a warm hotel room was waiting, I pressed on and was able to dry out my clothing to some satisfaction overnight. From Riva del Garda, it was a scenic ride across the Alps at Brenner Pass, then to Innsbruck. This picture-perfect town was the last stop before the tour ended back in Munich—just in time to celebrate the first day of *Oktoberfest* on the Theresienwiese, a fitting climax for toasts all around among the riders, Michael, and Rudy our mechanic, imbibing the delicious "fresh" beer in one of the many beer tents. That *Oktoberfest* was the perfect finale to my reading that magazine article nine months earlier in Hong Kong: *Europe, a Motorcycle, and You.*

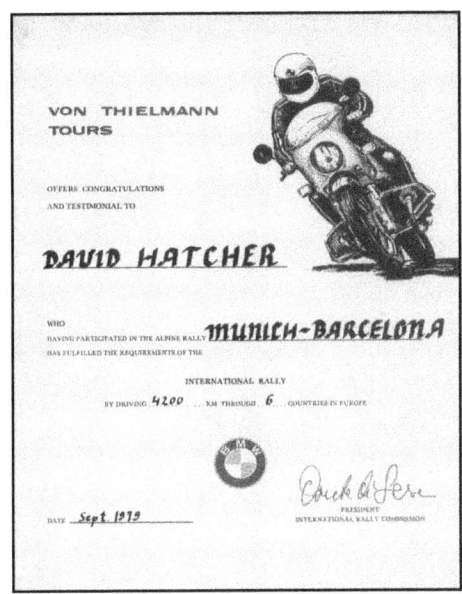

Certificate, Completion of VonThielmann Motorcycle Rally.

And as the Germans love to say in all of the beer tents at *Oktoberfest,* "Wunderbar!" "Ein prosit." "Gemütlichkeit."

Munich Oktoberfest.

\# \# \#

## CHAPTER 13

From Oktoberfest In Munich to the Crisis of Starvation Among Cambodian Refugees, October–November 1979

AFTER SAYING GOODBYE to my new motorcycling friends, I landed in Bangkok just as the refugee situation along the Thai-Cambodian border was becoming a major international story. A famous visitor that October was Leo Cherne, chairperson of the International Rescue Committee, who told reporters upon his arrival in Bangkok that "In Cambodia today, the living envy the dead." How sad and true.

In the months since the invasion of Cambodia by large numbers of PAVN (Peoples' Army of Vietnam—the North Vietnamese Army), the Chinese-backed Khmer Rouge melted away rather than attempt to battle the PAVN advance anywhere inside the country. Thousands of civilian followers held captive by the Khmer Rouge had been pushed ever closer to the Thai border. The starving and pathetic Cambodians, mostly women and children, were spending nights in the rugged jungles and forests along

the border with little food or water. They were shepherded virtually everywhere by armed Khmer Rouge minders.

Khmer Rouge soldiers on patrol, 1979.

On one visit we made, the Thai military had begun to load arriving
refugees onto buses for transfer to a new camp being set up to handle the
overflow. Many adult refugees had far-off looks of confusion and dislo-
cation. They had no idea on the number of days they had been roaming
around western Cambodia, utterly lost and destitute, with their fates and
futures in the hands of others.

I ended my television report for CBS that day saying: "None of these
refugees seem very sure of where they've been—or where they're going."

Reporters visited the border very frequently looking for new developments. Our crew rented a house in Aranyaprathet to have guaranteed lodging in case hotel space became very scarce. On one visit to a remote jungle
location, our crew came upon American Ambassador Morton Abramowitz

and Deputy Ambassador Burt Levin, accompanied by embassy refugee officials. It was highly unusual to find both senior diplomats away from the embassy at the same time, a signal of the American government's focus on the nature and magnitude of the suffering.

Earlier that day, we observed Thai soldiers who were providing what little dignity they could to dispose of several dozen Cambodian corpses in makeshift mass graves.

Thai soldier overseeing burial of corpses of Cambodian victims.

None of us had any knowledge of the specific and tragic consequences in the cursed country "where the living envy the dead", Internaional Rescue Committee Chairperson Leo Cherne was always saying.

Two excellent international photojournalists, Phillip Jones Griffith and David Burnett, were among reporters finding scenes like this one. It was not surprising to witness simple and starving peasants forced into a real-life death march, wandering along the dirt roads, and the occasional adult refugee so weakened, lying on the side of the road, waiting to die.

Cambodian adult waiting to die.

These thousands of Cambodian peasants were unknown to the outside world.

One Cambodian refugee who became well known to the outside world was Dith Pran, the subject of the movie *The Killing Fields*. Before 1975 he had worked alongside *New York Times* correspondent Sydney Schanberg. When Phnom Penh fell, Pran and his family were left behind, as portrayed in the movie. He showed up at the border in October 1979, without any family members. Refugee officials learned of his identity and relayed that information to the *New York Times*. Once Schanberg learned of Pran's survival and escape, Schanberg flew to Thailand to sign sponsorship paperwork for Pran's entry into the US.

I had the good fortune to interview Schanberg in an unusual location: the barbershop of the five-star Siam Intercontinental Hotel in Bangkok. He left for the border right afterwards to unite with Pran.

Within another week or two, everyone learned about a probable reason for Ambassador Abramowitz's personal trip to the border. The Carter administration announced that first lady Rosalynn Carter would represent her husband's administration to demonstrate the US commitment to support relief efforts for all refugees from South Vietnam, Laos, and Cambodia.

Thailand had recently opened a new camp facility in an open field near Sa Kaeo, approximately twenty-five miles from the border. Heavy monsoon rains had turned the camp into a muddy hellhole, an absolutely wretched place. Personal hygiene among the refugees was nearly impossible. Volunteers and medical personnel from many countries and organizations were joining the effort to do what they could.

Into this camp Rosalynn Carter strode one morning, joined by her White House staff and a handful of American congresswomen.

One of the photographers sent from Hong Kong to cover her visit was Hugh Van Es. Hugh became famous in 1975 for the historic photograph in Saigon of the desperate climb by Americans and South Vietnamese civilians to board a hovering helicopter one day before the surrender of South Vietnam.

Van Es was just a teenager from the Netherlands when he went to South Vietnam in 1968 as a television soundman for NBC News. He quickly joined the AP bureau's photographers' staff covering the war. His English was very, very rudimentary. He expanded his vocabulary by memorizing and mimicking the patois of American soldiers on numerous fire bases. The patois was of course laced with profanity. By the time Mrs. Carter arrived in Thailand, Van Es's speaking was replete with several off-color adjectives.

Mrs. Carter planned to visit the large open-air emergency hospital. Doctors and nurses were trying to cope with the needs of dozens of Cambodian women and small children. Both sides of the long canvas tent were raised during the day in a futile effort to allow circulation and cooling in a squalid camp. Everyone was forced to endure the daily heat and humidity.

A crush of photographers and video cameramen staked out positions along one side of the hospital, extending from the first half of the tent, where Mrs. Carter would enter, to the second half of the long tent. Van Es had chosen a location on the outside of the second half.

Mrs. Carter began her walk-through, viewing suffering women and tiny, emaciated children. She paused often, allowing the photographers and video cameramen their best chances for lasting images. Reporters were able to record her comforting words and, at times, audible gasps. When she reached the second half of the long tent, she was nauseous from the heat and stench. She began to walk towards the back of the tent. She ignored Van Es as he sweated and kneeled. Desperate to get his own photographs, he took his chance.

"How about this baby, Mrs. Carter?" he blurted out in his familiar gravelly voice.

"My, don't you boys have enough photos?" Mrs. Carter replied.

"Not in this f—in' gang bang!" Van Es replied.

She recovered her poise from his crude remark, bent over, and posed with the mother and child Van Es had chosen. He had his pictures and had just reinforced his reputation as a not-so-eloquent speaker of the English language. (Hugh Van Es passed away from a brain aneurysm in Hong Kong in 2009.)

The border story and the ongoing arrival of more refugees had one of the top spots in newsrooms all over the world. I was terribly busy reporting for CBS and *Newsweek* in New York and the BBC in London. My photo agency contact, Ernie Boehm at *Photoreporters*, was excited to promote and sell my continuing stream of photographs.

I also learned about the phenomenon among journalists called "big-footing," where reporters with much larger repuations in a news organization were sent in to cover stories. Local reporters like me were bypassed or reduced to reporting less significant details in what were known as sidebars.

One such CBS correspondent who big-footed me was Ed Bradley. He was not only compiling notes for *60 Minutes* but was also involved in the daily reporting for the *CBS Evening News*. Another big-footer a few years later was Steve Kroft, in India.

With such a hectic and continuing news situation, I became my own assignment editor with close friends in addition to filing my own stories. I contracted work and paid fees to capable friends like Vicky Butler. We met three years earlier in Bangkok. She was teaching English in a Thai university but wanting to branch out to do reporting. She went on to marry the well-known diplomat at the American embassy, Timothy Carney. She would accompany him in his future State Department postings as ambassador to Haiti and to Sudan, and as a senior diplomat for reconstruction in post–Saddam Hussein Iraq, inter alia. Tim was a consummate diplomat.

But just as soon as the story reached the top of the daily international news diet, it quickly lost its priority status with assignment editors everywhere. Iranian followers of Ayatollah Khomeini stormed the American embassy in Tehran and took fifty-two diplomats and embassy staff hostages. They were held for four hundred and forty-four days until the inauguration of President Reagan in January 1981.

#   #   #

CHAPTER 14

American Hostages in Iran, Soviet Red Army Landing in Kabul—Hatcher Left Out, November–December 1979

THE TAKEOVER OF the American embassy in Tehran and the incarceration of the fifty-two American diplomats superceded all other stories, understandably. Our story of starving Cambodians caught in the proxy war between the Soviet Union and China lost its prominent standing.

The Soviet Union wasted little time taking advantage of the world's focus on Iran. On Christmas Eve, Soviet Red Army troops landed in Kabul and claimed victory over an existing Communist government.

I was on my first Christmas leave in the US since 1975. While the Soviet Red Army was establishing control in Kabul, several news reporters found out that they would be allowed into Kabul during the chaotic transfer of power. My close friend and CBS cameraman Derek Williams received a visa. He linked up in Kabul with CBS News correspondent Don Kladstrup, who had flown in from Europe. They recorded videotape of the expanding military occupation in Kabul and other street scenes before the authorities put all the Western reporters under house arrest, forbidding further movement around Kabul.

Within days all Western reporters were ordered to leave. Derek and Don stopped in Pakistan and participated in a live satellite broadcast into the *CBS Morning News*. At one point in the interview, Don's earpiece came out, rendering him unable to hear Bob Schieffer's question from New York. Schieffer recognized Don's accidental hearing loss and quickly tossed same question to Derek. He had chilled out, since he thought the question would be coming to Don. Taken aback, when Schieffer asked him about his overall impressions of life in Kabul, Williams blurted out, "In the streets, the people are staying at home." A comment that would make the late Yogi Berra proud. We at CBS and other journalist friends gave Derek a friendly roasting when he told us in Bangkok of his brilliant answer.

Compared to the focus on many Asian stories in the latter half of the 1970s, the first year of the 1980s paled. I managed to stay busy enough to earn sufficient income from my three major news outlets.

Allow me to pause briefly here to describe my payment arrangements with some small variations with all three news organizations.

As a CBS radio stringer from 1976 until 1981, I was encouraged to offer radio stories *on speculation* as frequently as possible. On days I would file, that would be one or two, and rarely three stories, usually less than a minute each. If the radio editors in New York decided to broadcast a story either on the radio network or offer the story to those stations for their individual decisions on using I would be paid.

If editors initiated the request, for one or more stories, I was paid without fail.

For each story broadcast on the hourly updates on the full network, I was paid thirty dollars, to include flagship broadcasts on *CBS World News Roundup* (morning) and *CBS World News Tonight* (evening). For stories sent down to the stations to decide, regardless of how many might run the story, I was paid sixteen dollars.

For daily work as a field producer on any television story, usually as a substitute soundman, I was paid seventy-five dollars per day for the number of days on that story, plus payment for normal living expenses anywhere outside Bangkok. When our staff reporter, Peter Collins, was absent and CBS asked me to cover a story for television, I was paid the same amount.

The BBC had a different schedule for payments. *BBC World Service* shortwave news broadcasts went all over the world, in twenty-seven languages. All language services in London could decide individually to pay for the story and translate it into one or more languages. I was paid sixteen pounds sterling per story. The exchange rate in 1977 equalted approximately seventy-five US dollars; later, the British pound dropped in value: the amount was around forty-five dollars.

The BBC also had a daily roundup called *Twenty-Four Hours* in the late afternoon, London time. If editors wanted that show's anchor to engage me in a live two-way discussion, I was paid a different amount, up to twenty-four pounds sterling.

The BBC agreed to pay me a small monthly retainer, in the amount of $200. Any time the monthly total of payments from stories exceeded that amount, I was paid the retainer plus the difference. The BBC almost never assigned me to assist any of its visiting television correspondents. Those correspondents often treated me to an occasional meal or drinks for information that would be helpful to their stories.

Newsweek was different as well. Assignments either from Hong Kong or New York were in the form of an expected story length, to determine the number of days in any week. For stories up to five hundred words, normally for another reporter's byline, I could charge for two days at a rate of seventy-five dollars per day.

If the editors wanted longer accounts, and there was the possibility of adding my name to the byline on any story, the story length would be in the neighborhood of 750 to 1,000 words, and I could charge for three or four days' effort. On any likely cover story, or for helping when any correspondent was sent to Thailand for the story, I was always paid for four full days, for each week's efforts, regardless of word count in my filing.

Newsweek usually paid any legitimate or quasi-legitimate expenses I incurred in my reporting, to include entertainment of sources to gather information, or travel expenses for trips outside the capital, regardless of distance or destination.

I was also contacted occasionally by other news services for infrequent contributions, with a fixed pay rate agreed upon beforehand, mostly from the Canadian Broadcasting Corporation for its *Sunday Morning* magazine program (a weekly world summary) and once by the *Toronto Globe and Mail* to cover a trial in 1983 of a Canadian citizen charged with drug trafficking.

CHAPTER 15

Into the Decade of the 1980's: Big Changes and More Alpine Riding, 1980

MIDWAY IN 1980, the PAVN, the Peoples' Army of Vietnam, pushed the Khmer Rouge close enough to the Thai border that Vietnamese artillery rounds were landing in Thailand, creating a significant international incident. It was the first time that we could remember when Communist Vietnam used artillery to damage property on the Thai side of the border. My cameraman, driver, and I once had to take cover behind our car on a lonely dirt road while a small number of rounds landed around us. Luckily that barrage ended without any damage or any threats to our personal safety.

The annual *ASEAN* foreign ministers meeting (*ASEAN* is the Association of Southeast Asia [noncommunist] nations) was taking place in Kuala Lumpur, Malaysia a few days later. *Newsweek* sent me to cover the public sessions. The day I arrived, I was able to contact the Thai foreign minister. I mentioned that I had just been to his country's border to witness the shelling by the Vietnamese artillery howitzers. He invited me to his hotel suite for a debriefing. The next day, during the joint press conference, he told everyone present about the border shelling and attributed the details to me.

A couple of months later, I was off to Europe to join that year's Alpine tour with old and new riders. A few of us made a day trip to the famous town of Salzburg to enjoy the city life and vistas of Mozart's birthplace.

That year's tour destination on the Mediterreanean was the walled city of Dubrovnik, a World Heritage Site and thirteenth-century seat of maritime power in what is now Croatia. On that trip we rode from Munich through eastern Austria, to include the stunning mountain pass near the Grossglockner Mountain, 3,800 meters at its peak, or approximately 12,400 feet. We crossed into Yugoslavia and passed the picturesque Lake Bled, with the famous Assumption of Mary island pilgrimage church, before riding several delightful days along the rocky coastal highway along the Adriatic Sea.

Mountain pass Della Stelvio, Austria-Italy.

Our first major city in Croatia was Split, with its memorable waterfront architecture. We continued to Dubrovnik the next day. We often encountered extremely high winds buffeting our motorcycles on the coastal highway: *sirocco winds*, hot desert winds blowing northward from the Sahara Desert and across the Mediterranean.

The Dalmatian coastline was dotted with numerous small fishing villages. One in particular, named Biograd (and not the Serbian capital of

Belgrade), accommodated me in a quaint restaurant inside a natural cave to consume a delicious lunch.

Another beautiful town on the way was Makarska, near the city of Sarajevo, the embattled capital of Bosnia and Herzegovina, and Mostar. I did not take the time to explore either, preferring to ride on to Dubrovnik. I thoroughly enjoyed exploring many of the narrow streets inside the walls of the city.

After our forty-eight-hour stay in Dubrovnik, we rode back to Split to start the return part of the trip back to Munich. At Split we boarded an overnight ferry to Ancona, Italy, on the Adriatic coast. With our motorcycles tied down on board, we partied into the wee hours in the ship's nightclub, joining other passengers.

From Ancona we rode northward and then turned east, skirting Venice and heading to the tiny fishing port of Grado, near the border crossing of Trieste. Grado seemed to be largely unaffected by major tourist waves. Several delightful seafood restaurants dotted the downtown's few streets.

We were able to visit Venice during the next day, before turning northward into the Dolomite Alps of northern Italy. We spent a few hours in the well-known ski resort of Cortina d'Ampezzo, the site of the 1956 Winter Olympics. The very scenic roads in the Dolomites made for spectacular riding with numerous switchbacks before we crossed into eastern Austria and started back toward Munich.

Enjoying ripening grapes in a vineyard along the route.

Once back in Munich, we stored the motorcycles and spent the next afternoon just as we had the previous year, at *Oktoberfest*. I said goodbye the following day to all the riders on the tour, old and new, and tour organizer Michael.

Little did I know that the next few days back in Bangkok would bring about a dramatic change in my life. In short, I fell in love.

But first, I received a well-deserved lesson in humility. It happened during a birthday party for fellow journalist Rodney Tasker, another foreign correspondent who, like John McBeth, worked for the *Far Eastern Economic Review*, an excellent regional weekly magazine. Rodney's party was held in one of the raucous go-go bars in Bangkok and was little more than a gathering of Rodney's closest colleagues to toast to his longevity and to all-around good health and happiness for many of us.

That evening, in the large Super Star bar on the infamous Patpong Road, the usual mix of resident expat customers was supplemented by a dozen or more young American sailors on R&R in Bangkok. All were having a good time enjoying the music and the dancing. One of the sailors set down his drink on the bar, walked up to me, and asked nonchalantly, "What do you do?"

Well, with a few of my close friends standing next to me, yours truly took a deep breath, swelled up his chest, and affected his most resonant, full-throated baritone voice and said, "I'm a reporter here for CBS News. You've probably seen me on TV or heard some of my radio reports back in the States."

The sailor was at first somewhat confused, then nonplussed, and blurted out, "Oh, I thought you worked on my ship," and turned around and walked away! Humility is certainly one of our greatest virtues, just as false pride is one of mankind's—and mine, at the time—greatest sins.

Now, back to the budding romance about to hit me right in the face.

# # #

## CHAPTER 16

The Lady with Whom I Decided to Spend the Rest of My Life, October 1980— Till Death Do Us Part

DURING THE TOUR in Europe, I thought about buying a recent European automobile and had fantasized about something flashy like a late-model BMW convertible.

Back in Bangkok, I asked our former CBS News secretary for any close friends of hers who were car sales representatives. She immediately mentioned a friend of hers who was the sales manager at the local Volvo dealership. Not that I was looking for a family sedan typical of the Volvo line but merely to find a dealership offering recent model used Japanese automobiles. I scaled back my fantasy over a BMW convertible.

When I arrived at the Volvo dealership, I climbed the flight of stairs to the second-floor offices. Several office workers worked at desks along the floor-to-ceiling windows looking down upon the open showroom below.

The first desk was unoccupied; apparently the receptionist was temporarily away. The lady at the second desk was very cute and seemed to want to help me.

For some strange reason, I blurted out an expression not in Thai or in English but in Lao and the sister dialect from northeast Thailand, asking her, "Do you speak Lao?" To which she immediately replied in a mix of Thai and Lao, "Don't speak." I told her in Thai that I had come to see the sales manager. I had a hard time taking my eyes off of her when she whirled around to see if the sales manager was in his office.

He came out of his office, introduced himself, and proceeded to allow me to test drive one of the few Japanese cars currently on the used car lot. I was not tremendously impressed and thanked him, all the while trying to think up a good reason for returning soon—if only to renew my fleeting acquaintance with the charming young lady in the office.

A few days later, I called and asked the sales manager to show me another car on the lot. He did, and the same protocol applied, only this time, the receptionist at the first desk saw me coming as she looked down through the floor-to-ceiling window. Before she could warn the object of my affection to avoid me by fleeing to the safety of an unoccupied office, I ambushed her before she could disappear. She politely acknowledged my arrival and passed the word to the sales manager.

He tactfully coaxed me into driving a Volvo 244 DL, larger than what few Japanese cars were on the lot. From the first moment in frenetic Bangkok traffic, I was impressed by the solid handling and the comfortable feel of the Volvo. I said nothing, other than ask the sales manager about the female object of my attention. He said her name was Vasana (meaning "Opportunity" in Thai). And I asked him if he might suggest getting to know her better in a "safe" social occasion. He might have thought about the nice commission if he could put both sides together: my purchase of the Volvo 244 DL, whether or not anything came from my embryonic infatuation with Vasana.

The sales manager read my mind and suggested that I return in a day or two and invite both of them out for lunch. She might well refuse to have lunch without an escort.

That lady wrote her own version of those days of budding romance:

> *Dave had a very strong and deep voice and confused me when he spoke not in English, nor in my native language, but in the dialect from Laos spoken by Thai people in the northeast part of my country. He asked me, "Do you speak Lao?" in that regional dialect. I was confused, and all I could say was one word in that dialect and one word in Thai—coming out in English, "Don't speak."*
>
> *I quickly called the sales manager from his office to take over. I found out that Dave had been referred to come and ask by name for the sales manager; Dave wanted to see if there were any recent-model Japanese cars on the lot.*
>
> *A few days later, he returned to talk to the sales manager again. My office girlfriend spotted Dave through the large window that looked down on the open-air showroom below. She told me that the same* farang *(foreigner) was coming.*
>
> *I jumped up and ran to hide in a nearby office, but I was too slow.*

Vasana, 1981.

I agreed after that meeting to have lunch with Dave, but only in the presence of our escort, the sales manager.

Long story short—six months later, after that chance meeting in my office, and after a growing friendship, this gossip item appeared in the English-language newspaper Bangkok Post:

Bachelor about town, West Point graduate and FCCT President Dave Hatcher of CBS News is looking forward to sharing married life with pretty Vasana Chinbutr (FCCT was Foreign Correspondents Club of Thailand.)… The two met when Dave went to buy a car at the Volvo showroom where his bride-to-be works. Love started to blossom, and the chance meeting has now led to marriage, despite friends' joking remarks that "she came with the car."

Yes, Dave ended up buying a recent-model Volvo, not a Japanese car, and allowed me to drive the car occasionally, especially to my parents' home or for other occasional sightseeing excursions outside Bangkok.

Our wedding in July 1981 was an all-day affair, beginning before dawn and lasting to the full wedding reception in the evening.

One of Dave's close Thai friends of ten years, who owned a successful jewelry export business to high-end department stores around the world, had written a letter to Dave's parents saying that Dave had asked them to serve as surrogate parents for the wedding. The letter said in part:

> *My wife and I had met Miss Vasana Chinbutr many times and got to know her very well, and we both have had the opportunity to meet her parents and parents' friends recently. They all feel that David and Vasana will be a perfect couple, my wife and I agree because they love each other very much and are ready to get marriage [sic]… we have known David for many years, and I always feel that he is my younger brother. I hope that you will agree with us about David's plan.*
>
> > *On that sixth day of July, from the duplex that I shared with my older sister and her family, the first stop in the morning was a hospital in Bangkok providing healthcare for Buddhist monks.*

The first activity at the hospital was a small prayer service, all in Thai, for us and another couple unknown to us but scheduled for the same time. From that prayer service, our wedding party moved to the wards with several injured or sick Buddhist monks occupying hospital beds. Dave and I presented care packages of grooming items and personal-care products to symbolize our desire to serve others.

Our wedding day preceded the huge royal wedding in London a few weeks later, of Prince Charles to Diana Spencer, the princess-in-waiting. In advance of that wedding, CBS bureaus around the world had been asked to send in video coverage of weddings elsewhere in the world to compare with the royal wedding in London. Dave's CBS camera and sound colleagues followed us throughout the day. Dave thought that CBS would schedule video from Bangkok and unique Thai cultural aspects and native-style clothing as appropriate into other weddings around the world.

From the monks' hospital we moved across town to Wattana Church, started decades earlier by the American Presbyterian Missionaries organization, for a small Christian ceremony. I changed into a white bridal gown and felt very special walking down the aisle with my father and joining Dave and others as the American pastor read the famous words of matrimony and pronounced us as man and wife.

The next activity was restricted to the two of us and parents or surrogate parents, at a famous Chinese restaurant serving a traditional dim sum meal sponsored by Dave's surrogate parents.

The other intimate ceremony of the day, a lustral (holy) water pouring ceremony, took place in the early evening before the reception. I had humbly asked the owner of the Volvo franchise, a respected former judge, to lead my parents, Dave's surrogate parents, and the small wedding party to pour lustral water over the hands of the two of us, with our hands linked *by a small special cord, as we knelt before the others to accept the symbolic anointing and to receive the blessings of our dearest relatives and closest friends.*

Engagement party.

Wedding photo of Mrs. David Hatcher.

Lustral water pouring ceremony.

The reception followed in the main part of the Foreign Correspondents'
Club of Thailand clubhouse. Many of Dave's journalist colleagues, from many
countries, showed up. Many of my close friends from childhood, Bangkok Com-
mercial College, and my early adult years showed up, along with numerous close
friends and business associates of my mother and father.

Our honeymoon was unfortunately put on hold by Dave's unexpected
professional obligations. Our daily routines resumed, mine at the Volvo office and
Dave's reporting for CBS News and the BBC and staying in contact with another
news outlet, Newsweek magazine. (Dave was very busy all the time.)

# # #

## CHAPTER 17

A Honeymoon Bifurcated by New Zealand and Apartheid in South Africa—July 1981

"HAVEN'T YOU READ," (Jesus) replied, "that at the beginning the Creator 'made them male and female,' and said, 'For this reason a man will leave his father and mother and be united to his wife, and the two will become one flesh' (Matt. 19:4–5).

After several years as a young man, eschewing some of the Bible's best teachings on maturity and engaging for over a decade in a bachelor lifestyle marked by wine, women, and song after West Point, I had begun to alter that lifestyle and live up to Proverbs 22:6: "Train up a child in the way he should go, and when he is old, he will not depart from it."

I'm sure my parents prayed over this verse for each of their three children, perhaps especially for me. The enormous philosophy within that one verse would come to reveal itself increasingly over the next few years, thanks be to God.

The aforementioned circumstances Vasana mentioned that caused us to postpone our honeymoon for a few weeks were because CBS assigned our crew to fly to New Zealand to cover an exhibition tour featuring two of the world's best national rugby teams: the Springboks from South Africa and the host New Zealand All Blacks.

The reason for the world's focus: South Africa had just placed its first-ever Black citizen, 30-year-old Errol Tobias, on its national rugby team, in the country condemned by the civilized world for its notorious apartheid policy. The attention within the entire British Commonwealth grew into a major international story, especially among founding Commonwealth members: United Kingdom, Canada, Australia, New Zealand, Irish Free State, South Africa, and Newfoundland, a dominion of the British Empire before becoming a Canadian province in 1949.

The *Sydney (Australia) Morning Herald* wrote during the tour, "Foreign critics call Tobias a token black, but there is no question that the deceptive and strong inner back is a merit selection in the formerly all-white Springbok side." The article quoted Tobias as saying, "People are entitled to their opinions, but I have no complaints. Nothing has happened to make me believe that I am (being) used by anyone."

With that background, our crew flew into Auckland and made our way out to the first city of the tour: Gisborne on the east side of the North Island, facing the South Pacific Ocean. Gisborne bills itself "the first city to see the sun"—the first large community in Asia that is west of the International Date Line.

Our crew included four of us. Besides me, the two gentlemen already familiar to readers, Misters Derek Williams and Dexter Leong, and CBS Asia bureau chief Paul Byers, based in Hong Kong. A bit of biographical information on these three. Paul was an American citizen and had become Asia bureau chief after Brian Ellis was promoted to foreign editor in New York City.

Derek was a New Zealand citizen from the South Island. His father and grandfather were Anglican clergy. The bishop of the Anglican Diocese realized Derek's father's gifts and talents in resuscitating parishes, so he was often assigned to parishes with dwindling congregations or failing finances. Derek had joined CBS News a decade earlier in South Vietnam as a sound-man. He received a promotion to staff cameraman during our time together in Bangkok.

Dexter was an American-born Chinese (ABC) colleague who grew up in the Bay Area of California. He joined CBS a few years earlier as a sound-man for Norman Lloyd, an award-winning CBS News cameraman from Australia. Norman and Dexter came to Thailand in 1979 to augment the network's covering of the Cambodian refugee crisis. Soon after that assignment, Dexter asked for a transfer to Bangkok to become Derek's soundman.

In New Zealand, winter was just beginning. We decided to do a bit of clothes shopping on that Saturday morning, mostly for an extra sweatshirt or woolen sweater and/or warm boots and warm socks.

The morning of the exhibition match, we decided to split up but agreed to meet an hour or so later at a popular pub near a few clothing stores. At the designated time, Paul and I wandered into the pub and thought Derek and Dexter would be close behind. After several minutes, we became concerned when the other two still had not shown up.

Derek and Dexter entered one section of the pub where the locals were partying early for the All Blacks. "I remember Derek and I entering and pulling up to the bar and ordering a beer," Dexter said. "I sensed some tension right away. After a while it was apparent this was not the right pub, so we left and wandered about until we found the other doorway."

Dexter said that after a bit, some locals in the new section asked where both of them had been. He and Derek admitted to having been in the other section, surrounded by Māoris. The locals in the new section were amazed and replied, "You walked out of there alive?"

Now, the rest of the story. Derek said that pubs in many cities in New Zealand were largely divided by economics. Paul and I had entered the Lounge Bar (slightly more upmarket) while Derek and Dexter unknowingly entered the Public Bar that served cheaper fare, and where both spent time waiting for Paul and me to show up.

Dexter also had Asian facial characteristics of mixed parentage; his real ethnicity was hard to judge at first impression. Since many of the customers in the Public Bar were Māoris, many apparently assumed he was Māori or part Māori. Only when someone happened to mention that the building contained two sections did Derek and Dexter walk out one door and into the other and reunite with us.

That would not be the first time Dexter was subject to confusion in other Asian counties over to the Indian subcontinent. Many local citizens in those countries, especially immigration officers, assumed Dexter might have one or both parents of the main ethnic group in that country he was entering. Often those officials would address him in the native language, possibly assuming that he was accompanying the Caucasian foreigners as an interpreter or field producer.

Once Dexter answered questions in his laid-back Bay Area English, officers usually realized that he was an American citizen and probably of limited or no fluency in that particular native language. If I remember correctly, this happened at least once in the following countries: Vietnam, Cambodia, Malaysia, India, Pakistan, the Philippines, and Sri Lanka.

We reunited at the pub in Gisborne in plenty of time to return to the hotel and proceed to the stadium. The biggest highlight for me, and probably for every visitor attending his or her first live sporting event involving a New Zealand team, was the passionate rendition of the Māori Haka dance, which, according to NewZealand.com, is "usually performed in a group and representing a display of a tribe's pride, strength, and unity. Actions include the stomping of the feet, the protrusion of the tongue and rhythmic body slapping to accompany a loud chant. The words of a haka often poetically describe ancestors and events in the tribe's history."

My emotions were captive to the moment described here—heart-throbbing and excitement from the dramatic choreography and singing by the entire team "attacking" the Springboks or any other foreign opponent.

The match went off without any incident, but the next match the following week in Hamilton did not. In fact, that match was called off because of organized protests beforehand.

Hamilton is located in the middle of the North Island, an hour and a half from Auckland. Our crew enjoyed a raucous night in a pub close to our hotel. None of the revelry by a great assortment of the Kiwi pub dwellers gave any hint, however, of the unusual protests that would unfold before the next day's scheduled match.

News media from many countries had arrived in Hamilton. Television crews, print reporters, and still photographers from all over the world witnessed the exposed politics of apartheid in South Africa against the principled stand for the future, whatever that would be, by the British Commonwealth.

The exhibition in New Zealand violated the spirit of the 1977 Gleneagles Agreement signed within the British Commonwealth. Presidents and prime ministers agreed to support an antiapartheid campaign, chiefly by discouraging any sporting competition with teams or individuals from South Africa.

The mood of the entire exhibition might have been summed up during the first press conference in Auckland upon the arrival of the Springbok team. An Australian reporter asked the Springbok coach if his only black player, Errol Tobias, had more freedom in New Zealand than all Black South Africans back home. The irony was not lost on the press corps for the entirety of the exhibition.

As the entire press contingent waited on or near the field at Hamilton during warm-ups, a crowd of more than three hundred demonstrators showed up just outside one end of the stadium and began to push on the stadium fence, which could not withstand the group's pressure. The fence crumpled. The entire group of demonstrators, supposedly including Māoris, Indigenous Aboriginal people from Australia, and possible minorities from other countries, flowed into the top row of seats and down onto the playing field.

Once on the playing field, most locked their arms in the middle of the field and adamantly stood their ground.

Unarmed New Zealand police surrounded the group but did not initiate any crowd-removal action, other than using loudspeakers to ask the demonstrators to disperse.

Most television crews and photojournalists were busy capturing the chaos and the international implications behind the protests.

Our crew was not spared physical confrontation. Cameraman Derek and soundman Dexter walked along the edge of the protestors. A short middle-aged Caucasian lady ran up behind Derek and jumped up to grasp the electronic cable between the camera and sound recorder. She obviously hoped to sever the connection and cut off video capabilities.

Hatcher came to the rescue. I was behind Dexter when the lady ran up and showed her intention. I ran up behind her. Her feet were slightly off the ground from holding onto the cable. I gave her a perfect basketball hip befitting an NBA All-Star power forward. My intervention sent her sprawling to the ground. Derek turned his head around in confusion to see why his camera had been jerked backward, but the cable connection was not affected.

A photographer from South Africa apparently managed to capture that quick takedown, but we never saw any photograph or photographs of that incident.

Meanwhile, a small single-engine plane was circling the field dropping harmless sacks of cooking flour onto the field.

Finally, the stadium announcer told the entire group that the match was being cancelled due to reports that someone had stolen another light plane that was nearing the stadium. Senior law enforcement feared potential violence and/or physical harm to anyone on the field. Everyone went away without seeing a world-class rugby match.

Our crew covered the next match in Palmerston North, another North Island city near Wellington, the lovely capital on the southern tip of the North Island. That match did take place amid scaled-down protests. CBS sent us back to our home bureaus after that match.

My brief exposure to rugby at the highest level, and the athleticism and toughness of the All Blacks, cemented my love affair as a newfound All Blacks fan. I will always have profound respect for a later generation captain, Richie McCaw, for his spectacular rugby career and for his public service since retirement as a helicopter pilot flying rescue missions.

Richie McCaw leads the All Blacks in a Māori Haka.

\#   \#   \#

CHAPTER 18

The Honeymoon Trip Around the World, Return to Bangkok for Assignment in Taiwan, September–November 1981

"In this same way, husbands ought to love their wives as
their own bodies. He who loves his wife will love himself"

—Eph. 5:28.

WITH OUR CREW'S return to Bangkok, Vasana and I could embark on
our honeymoon. In the next six weeks, we traveled completely around the
world. I had failed romances too numerous to count, with increasing levels
of passion after my first harmless affair at the same age with eleven-year-
old Carol Olson from my grandparents' hometown. She probably never
suspected my affection. I was more convinced than ever in 1981, at the age
of thirty-five, that I wanted to spend the rest of my life not only with Vasana
but also any offspring of that union.

I grew up in a midsize Methodist (later United Methodist) church in Sioux City. My parents were strong believers. Once on my own as a young adult, I had wandered away from the Lord to a prodigal's life.

Without realizing God's prevenient grace in courting Vasana, I embarked on that desired matrimonial goal. From my time at West Point and continuing for the next dozen years, I avoided all mention of matrimony to anyone before that unforeseen rendezvous overtaking my desire for a used car in Bangkok.

I began that decisive change to that lifestyle soon after, during my first midlife crisis. I reacted to that tug of His grace and mercy and was intent on obeying Romans 10:9: "If you confess with your mouth that Jesus is Lord and believe in your heart that God raised Him from the dead, you will be saved." Much more of my personal spiritual journey awaits the reader in future chapters.

Our honeymoon itinerary began with a flight of several hours to Hawaii. It was Vasana's first visit to the US, to spend two days with a former army colleague and fellow Mitrapab parachute jumper in Thailand. His continuing army career had led him to a joint service assignment at the US Pacific Command headquarters in Hawaii. We next flew to San Francisco and spent a day sightseeing there with Janice Leong, the sister of our CBS soundman in Bangkok, Dexter Leong. That was another first for Vasana, setting foot on the mainland of the US.

After those two prologue visits, our next stop was Denver and Vasana's first exposure to my family via my older sister. Carole's remarriage in 1978 had enlarged the family, from her life as a single parent with three young children, to a blended family with two more young children along with her new husband Roger. Within a day or two of our arrival, the real love affair with our family began—with the arrival of my parents: their first face-to-face encounter with Vasana and her personality marked by deference and humility. After a few days in Colorado and several affectionate moments with most of the Hatcher clan (my other sister, Cathy, lived in the Twin Cities), Vasana and I piled into the back seat of my father's car. The four of us set out for Sioux City and the rolling farmland of Iowa. The Heartland.

We spent several hours driving along I-80 through Nebraska farmland to the broad expanse of the Missouri River at Omaha, and then turned north on I-29 for the last hour or so to reach Sioux City. The next few days were a whirlwind of activity introducing Vasana to many lifelong family friends, which included a short, informal wedding reception at our family's church. My grandparents came up from tiny Nemaha, Iowa to meet their grandson's new bride from Thailand.

Everything was a new and strenuous adventure for her, rushing through four different American subcultures—Hawaii, San Francisco, Denver, and the Heartland—meeting many new people who did not speak her language. Her English was improving since my showing up in her life, but she still had feelings of inadequacy in English.

We said goodbye to my parents and grandparents and flew to New York to start the second major leg of our round-the-world honeymoon. That would involve flying from JFK Airport to Frankfurt, Germany, and connecting to Munich. We joined Michael Von Thielmann's Alpine tour, my third straight year. Ever the trooper, Vasana raised no real objections to riding on the back of my motorcycle for the next twelve days or so. (To this day she says she never revealed to her parents that she had ridden on the back of a motorcycle for so many days—even though I believe that no outsider sees "the real Europe" from a rental car or tour bus or airline flights with no exposure to the many colorful towns and quaint villages.)

The destination for that year's ride was the town of Pula, Yugoslavia, on the Istrian Peninsula just south of Trieste, Italy. The first day of the tour took us across the Inn River to the Austrian town of Shaerding.

The day was memorable for a wedding ceremony for two Americans I had met on tour two years earlier, John and Patsy Lowengreen of Tampa, Florida. John owned his own successful motorcycle dealership. Patsy was new to touring but loved the entire experience during that first year to the Mediterranean beach resort of Sitges, Spain, south of Barcelona. John and Patsy often rode with me during that first tour, once they realized that I had a working knowledge of German, French, Spanish, and Italian.

Unknown to me, Michael had alerted other riders that Vasana and I were on our honeymoon, so we shared almost equal billing as a second pair of newlyweds. The following day the group rode east to the charming international city of Vienna that revels in its Old-World history and charm.

One legitimate complaint Vasana had but rarely mentioned was the lack of Asian food, either her native Thai food or even Chinese cuisine. She had to put up with a diet heavy on European food, of course. She learned to order Austrian fried chicken or Italian pasta as often as she could for dinner. She usually survived at lunchtime on whatever salad that day's local restaurant or bistro offered.

The two of us made a special stop one Vienna evening to sit in the sidewalk café of the Hotel Sacher and enjoy its world-famous Sacher Torte. I was ticking off items on my bucket list before bucket lists became fashionable.

The tour group left Vienna and rode east to Hungary. We spent two nights in the capital of Budapest—*Buda* on the hilly part and *Pest* on the flat part, divided by the Danube River. Hungary was still behind the Iron Curtain at the time. During our tour one morning, the guide pointed out the famous Budapest Stock Exchange Palace, then closed. The stock exchange itself had been abolished in 1948; the Lenin Institute took over the majestic building. Our guide failed to mention the reason for the abandonment of the national investment center during Communist rule. The Hungarian government reinstated the stock exchange in 1990.

We spent two nights at Lake Balaton southwest of Vienna, en route to Croatia and the publicized destination of Pula. Lake Balaton is the biggest lake in central Europe, surrounded by vineyards, volcanic mountains, and thermal spa resorts. Vasana and I enjoyed time walking along the lakeside and patronizing the restaurants. We crossed paths with other tour members often.

We rode southwest through the major city of Zagreb, now the capital of Slovenia, and on to the publicized destination of Pula and its beautiful views of the Adriatic Sea. We then turned north into Italy, passing through Trieste and heading into the Dolomite Alps and the charming town of Cortina d'Ampezzo, my second time there in twelve months. Vasana loved shopping for souvenirs for parents and friends back in Thailand, mostly crafts from cottage industries turning out colorful items for household decoration.

We reentered Austria and spent one night in the picturesque town of Innsbruck, capital of the western state of Tyrol and site of the 1976 Winter Olympics. The town's name means "the bridge over the Inn (River)." Several days of riding had taken us back to the same Inn River of the first day's wedding celebration for John and Patsy Lowengreen at Schaerding, Austria.

Our last overnight stop before returning to Munich was the resort town of Hohenschwangau, almost spitting distance from the world-famous Neuschwanstein Castle built by King Ludwig II in the late nineteenth century.

That was a beautiful penultimate stop on our honeymoon through five countries and an unforgettable introduction for Vasana to culture-rich continental Europe. And about 1,500 miles of accident-free riding: nearly two weeks on the road without any sicknesses, stomach discomfort, or any other significant problems.

After putting my motorcycle in storage and escorting my bride to *Oktoberfest* with the entire group, the two of us extended our honeymoon slightly by taking the Deutsche Bahn train to Bonn to visit friends of ours from Bangkok, Kurt and Gertrude Hoefle. Kurt was the CBS staff cameraman in Bangkok until CBS transferred him to his native Germany in 1979. Neither he nor Gertrude knew Vasana, so it was a wonderful opportunity to reminisce and enjoy Thai food that Vasana fixed in the Hoefles' lovely townhouse in Bonn.

Kurt Hoefle, CBS News cameraman in Bangkok and Bonn.

Kurt asked me to help return a rental car from his most recent assignment for CBS—a new Mercedes sedan. I drove the Mercedes, and Kurt led in the family car; we drove to Cologne (Koln), a half hour from Bonn. The reason for my mentioning: I reached a speed of 200 kph, roughly 120 mph: a testament to the marvel of engineering on the autobahn and in a luxury German automobile. I knew that I would almost certainly never approach that speed again.

While in Bonn, CBS News contacted me through Kurt and asked me return to Bangkok and quickly transfer to Taipei, Taiwan. The country was celebrating the seventieth anniversary of Double Ten Day, Taiwan National Day, dating back to 1911. The Double Ten namesake commemorates the start of an uprising on October 10 and the collapse of the imperial Qing dynasty that led to the establishment of the Republic of China in early 1912.

Vasana resumes her account:

I never revealed to my parents that I had been on the back
of a motorcycle for nearly two weeks! Our trip took us through

the many picturesque towns and villages of central Europe, and
up and down numerous Alpine mountains and mountain passes.
Thank God that Dave was an excellent rider the whole
way before we returned to a much more normal life in Thailand.
This year marks our forty-third year of marriage.

Because of the need to have a reporter in Taipei, CBS upgraded the two of us to first class from Frankfurt to Bangkok to get me back in time. Another fantastic way to complete a magical round-the-world six-week honeymoon.

Several airlines, including Lufthansa, were equipping their Boeing 747s with special sleeping accommodations on long-haul flights. The upper compartment offered twin-sized beds. As first-class passengers, Vasana and I could avail ourselves of the sleepers at no charge for the twelve-hour nonstop flight to Bangkok.

Traveling first class as CBS News crew members in Asia became a wonderful perquisite that accountants in New York allowed with the introduction of electronic news-gathering equipment in the late 1970s. On any assignment that superiors in New York thought might last long enough to need editing and other special equipment for satellite transmissions to New York, ground staff of the airlines would normally chop off several hundred dollars in excess baggage fees—if our crew purchased first-class tickets for three or more passengers. Airline staff were not inclined, however, to heavily discount any fees for passengers traveling on economy fares (always a sore point among our print journalist colleagues when covering stories).

A running joke our crew always had when travel agents asked if we were flying first class, was, "Of course! Doesn't everybody?" On outgoing flights from Bangkok, lasting six hours or more, to destinations such as New Delhi, Karachi, or Colombo, Sri Lanka, with mostly after midnight arrivals, flying first class was a pleasant beginning to, and the even more pleasant return after, such an assignment.

My assignment in Taipei lasted less than a week and involved updating the general political situation with the Communist Government in Beijing.

On one day, the Taiwanese military flew a small group of journalists to the island of Quemoy very close to the mainland than Taiwan.

The Communist Chinese shelled Quemoy and its sister island of Matsu in the summer of 1958. Since then, Taiwan had greatly fortified both islands to protect its citizens there. The tour revealed many defensive preparations the Taiwanese military were always upgrading. I enjoyed the tour very much. The distance from the mainland was only one hundred miles; the Taiwan Strait or Formosa Strait was always considered a flashpoint in Asia.

I landed back in Bangkok after an absence of nearly two months. I learned that as president of the Foreign Correspondents' Club of Bangkok, I was going to preside over the dedication of new club premises in the upscale Oriental Plaza shopping center a few steps from the world-famous Oriental Hotel. The FCCT had its own premises in the Oriental Hotel before the late 1970s.

To dedicate the premises, club officers succeeded in issuing a formal invitation to the older princess in Thailand, HRH Sirindhorn. As club president, I welcomed the crown princess to officiate most of the short dedication ceremony. In truth, I was looking forward to ending my term as president upon the next round of elections for the coming year.

The final key event of 1981 was a trip with CBS to Pakistan. Our foreign desk in New York wanted coverage of Secretary of State Alexander Haig's visit to discuss developments in Afghanistan and policy implications for the US. CBS dispatched three crews to Islamabad, ours from Bangkok and others from Rome and Nairobi. CBS wanted to have crews present in Peshawar, Islamabad, and the Khyber Pass once the itinerary for Secretary Haig was released to the public.

Almost as soon as we arrived in Islamabad, news came that martial law had been declared in Poland, causing Secretary Haig to cancel his trip to Pakistan. I would have no chance to speak directly to Secretary Haig and see if he would remember our crossing paths at West Point and my slightly inebriated misfortune with the glee club at the New York Athletic Club my senior year. But I never had the chance.

The three crews waited on standby in Islamabad until we could make return reservations to our home stations. We all departed the next day without any work to justify the expense CBS had incurred in sending three crews into Pakistan.

One of the very few lighthearted moments during that aborted trip came the night of our arrival in Karachi before we transferred to a domestic flight for the two-hour journey to Islamabad. Since Karachi was our first port of entry in the country, Pakistani customs had to clear all our equipment. Each crew traveled with several hundred pounds of gear. The three crews arrived almost together, in the middle of the night, and created chaos for the dozens of sleepy baggage tenders (skycaps). With numerous pieces of heavy electronic gear needing to be moved from customs and immigration booths to the domestic side of the airport, the skycaps were befuddled.

The skycaps' manager sized up the situation and began to order individual skycaps to assist members of each crew. The manager turned to Mario Biasetti, a Rome-based veteran cameraman for CBS, who was standing behind all his equipment, and shouted at Biasetti, "Take that man! Take that man!" as the manager pointed to one of the skycaps.

Veteran cameraman Biasetti had a priceless sense of humor. In a mocked falsetto voice, he hollered back, "He's not my type! He's not my type!" to guffaws from all the rest of us.

The tumultuous year of 1981 was drawing to a close, a year of profound change, the biggest of which was my marriage to a lady with whom I had decided to spend the rest of my life—and I am.

# # #

## CHAPTER 19

Time Out for Two Brief Assignments in the Philippines, 1982

IN JANUARY 1982, our crew flew to Manila to cover the first annual Manila International Film Festival, a brainchild of First Lady Imelda Marcos. She wanted to give the Philippine capital the prestige of having its own annual film festival, the first in Asia.

One of the first releases shown at the film festival was Peter Weir's great movie *Gallipoli*, starring Mel Gibson in one of his first major roles, about the tactical failures of the British and Australian forces in trying to defeat the Turkish enemy in World War I.

Two months earlier, in the rush to construct a gaudy new center as the permanent home for the film festival, faulty construction led to the collapse of scaffolding that buried more than one hundred workers under quick-drying cement. The building rush continued without pause, under fierce pressure from Imelda to have the center ready for the gala opening and many luminaries who would attend.

Workers had been unable to complete the rear wall of the building. They were ordered to build barriers near the rear wall to keep photographers from learning about the rushed and slipshod construction.

Among the international dignitaries were American film star George Hamilton and the President of the Motion Picture Association of America, Jack Valenti. One of the more cynical members of the press corps, Kevin Sinclair of the *South China Morning Post* (Hong Kong) typed up a satirical lead sentence that never saw print, something similar to, "Tonight the cream of Filipino society danced on the graves of a hundred unnamed construction workers who were sacrificed to satisfy First Lady Imelda Marcos's fixation on her legacy."

The next weekend, First Lady Imelda presided over the dedication of the new International Lung Center in the Philippines. We decided we would attend the occasion to see if Mrs. Marcos might say something newsworthy to us. Her older daughter Maria Imelda, nicknamed Imee, had eloped the previous month to Washington, DC, where she secretly married Filipino businessman Tommy Manotoc.

President and Mrs. Marcos were strongly opposed to the elopement. During the interim, the government spokespersons made the claim, without evidence, that unknown people had kidnapped Manotoc, possibly holding him for ransom. The story took on celebrity status with each passing day. Imee was back in circulation, but her new husband was not.

We had the chance to confront Mrs. Marcos in the center's ornate new lobby. I asked her if she knew the whereabouts of her new son-in-law. She blithely replied, "We hope he's in the Philippines!" and then scurried away behind her security guards. After a face-saving interval and without any real explanation, Manotoc reappeared and continued his job as the coach of a professional basketball team in the country.

The marriage did not last. Imee herself gradually immersed herself in a political career and rose to become a member of the Philippine Senate. Two and a half years later, I would sit alongside Imee on a five-hour trip to Bangkok from attending the funeral in New Delhi of Indira Gandhi. That unusual vignette is described later in the book.

The only other news assignment I had in the Philippines occurred during a time of increased public displeasure with the dictatorship of Ferdinand Marcos. He was trying to offset the growing popularity of one of his subordinates and possible rivals, General Fidel "Eddie" Ramos.

General Ramos at the time was the chief of the national constabulary (police force). Ramos would become president in the mid-1990s. He was a 1950 West Point graduate. I was fortunate enough during that visit to arrange an interview with General Ramos that happened shortly before an interview with President Marcos himself. Getting both interviews was a stroke of good luck and allowed me to compare the public strategies of both political rivals.

Two other memories survive from successive evenings of demonstrations against the US alliance with the Marcos regime. US Vice President George Bush had said, "We love your adherence to democratic principles and to the democratic processes," a quote that only added fuel to the fire of the protesters.

Metropolitan police had begun to disperse protesters one evening from outside the US embassy, setting off tear gas and chasing protesters away from the front of the embassy. Our crew tried to keep up with the police officers chasing the protesters through busy city streets.

I ran alongside one police officer who was firing his revolver while on the run, aiming at the protesters. As we ran down the street, I asked him if he worried about his bullets striking innocent bystanders. He said that his bullets were only for Communists!

The next afternoon, a similar protest pattern began in front of the US embassy. Our crew recorded images of the chaos as police again tried to disperse the protesters. No real damage or casualties occurred. The three of us returned to the Manila Hotel, the same hotel where Douglas MacArthur retained a large suite when he was the military advisor to the local government before World War II.

When I reached my room, I had an incoming call from producers of the *CBS Morning News* (readers may recall that Southeast Asia was roughly twelve hours ahead of East Coast time). The producers had blocked time for me to do a live voice interview with Diane Sawyer on the situation outside the embassy. The best quality audio connection was usually achieved by hooking up a pair of aluminum "alligator clips" from the audiocassette recorder to small leads inside the mouthpiece. This was done after unscrewing any standard three-piece telephone.

My challenge came when I noticed that the bedside telephone, and presumably most other bedside telephones in the hotel, were fabricated as one piece of a hard plastic with no way to disassemble either the mouthpiece or the earpiece and hook up the clips to the metal leads inside.

Then genius struck. Bathrooms in the elegant five-star hotel were equipped with standard phones and headsets. I was able to unscrew that mouthpiece and attach the clips to the aluminum leads there. News producers on the other end said the connection was very clear. Xanadu!

When the producers switched the program audio to Diane's voice on the phone, I fantasized that when she asked her first probable question, "What do you see now?", my answer would be: "Well, I see an ornate bathroom complete with the ornate bathtub I'm sitting on!"

But instead, I preferred to remain serious and do my best to paint a verbal picture for her viewers of the standoff that late afternoon.

I never had the opportunity to share that vignette face-to-face with Diane Sawyer.

# # #

## CHAPTER 20

Our First-Born Son and Trips Involving Afghan Mujahideen and Pow-Mia Hunters, 1983–1984

IN ADDITION TO the ongoing developments, including refugees escaping Vietnam, Cambodia, and Laos, and internal Thai political developments (a country that underwent numerous coups d'état since 1935), two major stories highlighted the year of 1983.

The first story involved an attempt by a former United States Army Special Forces officer and his small team to enter Laos to search for whom he believed were live Americans still held as prisoners of war. James "Bo" Gritz was one of a small coterie of Americans raising money in the US to launch efforts, supposedly heroic, to determine the possibility of live prisoners held against their will in Laos or Vietnam.

It was always a guessing game among the Bangkok press corps when trying to make sense of the claims of many of these Americans showing up from time to time. Sometimes these American fortune hunters allied themselves with former Laotian government officials.

One such former Lao official was a former major general in the Royal Laotian Army named Phoumi Nosavan. After two years of military education in France, he became the country's defense minister and a strongman in internal politics in the 1950s and early 1960s but was deposed and forced into exile in Thailand in 1965.

From his status under lenient house arrest in a Bangkok suburb, he and former loyal subordinates regularly contacted journalists to tout the chances of locating American prisoners. He once asked the US embassy for $100 million to extricate live Americans from Laos. Embassy officials, including military officers following all POW-MIA affairs, hardly took him seriously.

One of the most dramatic rescue attempts took place shortly after the New Year began. Jim Coyne, a close friend and investigative reporter for the magazine *Soldier of Fortune* brought me into his confidence regarding Bo Gritz and his efforts. The magazine was founded by a retired army lieutenant colonel named Robert Brown, a former Special Forces officer in Vietnam.

Coyne had learned from Brown's contacts that Bo Gritz had received substantial funding from Hollywood celebrities, including Clint Eastwood and William Shatner, to take a small team of other American adventurers into Laos.

Jim introduced me to one of Gritz's group who had become disillusioned. The venue for our meeting was a famous Bangkok bar, Lucy's Tiger Den, owned and managed by "Tiger" Rydberg, a retired American construction worker. His wife's nickname was Lucy.

The disillusioned former cohort revealed some details behind the first attempt a few months earlier, in November the previous year, to include some alleged funding for Gritz's efforts by the likes of Eastwood and Shatner.

Acting on a hunch, Coyne and I boarded the Sunday flight on the domestic airline to the Thai border town of Nakhon Phanom (NKP). NKP sits right on the Mekong River separating both countries. An American air base at NKP was formerly the site for launching rescue flights for downed American pilots in Laos and North Vietnam.

Jim and I spent that Sunday evening on the veranda of a lovely riverside café. We exchanged "Where you be, Bo?" shouts and laughed at the echoes as we both stared across the river.

On Monday morning, our driver dropped us off at the safe house that Gritz and his team had been using as their rear headquarters. Two of Gritz's support team, a man and a woman, were monitoring radio communications. We had no idea of exactly where Gritz and any members of his group were.

As we were talking to the two Americans, our driver raced back to the house with his horn honking and his lights blinking. He shouted excitedly that Bo Gritz had just walked into the provincial jail, a few kilometers away.

Our luck held. We jumped into the car and drove to the jailhouse. We were extremely lucky to find Gritz in a cell, in work pants and a simple T-shirt and looking as if he had not slept much. With him were two American compatriots, Scott Weekly and Gary Goldman. All three surrendered to the Thai police earlier that morning when crossing the river back in Thailand. They claimed that they had been in Laos for several days trying to begin searching for American prisoners. They never admitted to being lost. They probably were.

We videotaped comments made by the three, especially Gritz, and realized that we had a big story. Jim opted to stay in NKP for more intensive reporting for *Soldier of Fortune* magazine.

My Thai cameraman colleague Narong and I piled into the Toyota sedan for the ten-hour drive back to Bangkok; there were no airline connections that day. Upon our arrival back in Bangkok, we learned that a journalist competitor of mine, Mark Litke of ABC News, flew in from Tokyo to Bangkok and was on an unusual chartered flight to NKP in ABC's attempt to catch up and cover the story.

We encountered Mark and his crew at the satellite facility much later that evening. We observed their report and images as they were being uploaded to the satellite. Their story did not match ours for the drama of photographing the three incarcerated Americans upon their very first actual encounters with the police, or other major elements like the American couple at the safe house whom I could write into the drama.

Jim's investigative report a few weeks later became the definitive print story. It is still available online as "Operation Lazarus: The Inside Story" under the bylines of Jim Graves with Jim Coyne.

The trial in a provincial court for Gritz, Weekly, and Goldman, on charges of entering the country illegally, was held a few days later. Gritz showed up modeling his ribbon-laden khaki army uniform from prior service.

The Thai verdict declared all three as persona non grata (PNG) and required them to leave the country albeit with no further punishment, to my knowledge. I attended the trial to observe and provide radio reports to both CBS and BBC, and to be available on site if CBS wanted further video coverage of the story of the surrender.

One special note on personalities: our Thai driver Vichien. As a child and teenager growing up near the border in the 1940s, he was fluent in both languages. The Royal Thai Army commandeered him while he was still a minor, trained him in basic espionage and inserted him among the housekeeping staff of prominent Laotian officials in earlier decades.

Separate factions in the Laotian capital arrested him twice on suspicion of spying. The second time his imprisonment lasted so long that his mother and his Laotian wife gave him up for dead. He escaped, most likely at a time of political turmoil in Vientiane.

With the growing geopolitical alliance between the US and Thailand, he teamed up with an American navy veteran with many years of experience in South Vietnam. Both served together, albeit briefly, with hundreds of others, including Thai mercenaries, in the clandestine war against the Communist Pathet Lao and their North Vietnamese superiors. The American was Richard Armitage. He would feature prominently in American foreign policy positions in the coming years.

Hatcher and Vichien and Richard Armitage,
US State Department office, 2001.

Vichien became a great CBS resource as a field producer on many occasions when we required a second driver. He was also very persuasive with officials in the Ministry of Finance when anyone of us holding nonimmigrant visas needed to pay our annual Thai taxes. His negotiating tactics were almost always successful in lowering the amounts owed by all of us.

Because of our bond as former soldiers, our growing friendship, and his dependability, he became my closest Thai gentleman friend. I relied on him during our long wedding day for his helping at each stage of our wedding. He passed away in 2002 from liver cancer at the age of sixty-six.

My parents visited Vasana and me in Bangkok at Thanksgiving in 1982. Vasana and I flew back to the US with my parents to spend the Christmas holidays. The highlight for Vasana during that visit was her first time seeing snow up close, and lots of it. We were staying with my older sister's family in

Denver on Christmas Eve, when a major snowstorm struck the Denver area. During the next twenty-four hours, two feet of snow fell—an inch an hour.

Vasana's first time seeing snow, 1982.

After the roads around Denver were pretty much cleared, our parents and the two of us started the drive across eastern Colorado and Nebraska to spend New Year's Eve in Sioux City. Another blizzard hit the region as we crossed into Nebraska. Interstate 80 became exceedingly dangerous. We passed numerous semi-trailers and passenger cars stuck in the drifts. What normally was a long one-day drive took us three days. The first night on the road we were lucky to get one of the last motel rooms in the vicinity of North Platte.

The snowstorm seemed to be wreaking havoc all across the plains. I called the CBS radio desk in New York and volunteered to record and transmit two radio spots for their overnight use. They readily accepted. I checked with local law enforcement and TV stations for updates on the road conditions and estimates of continuing travel difficulties. Before midnight and with the other three trying to sleep, I called New York on the room's telephone, but without the benefit of an audiocassette recorder. I read the spots "live" into the phone without any mistakes, fortunately. My parents and wife were suitably impressed, if sleepily.

I still have the daily CBS radio logs showing both of my reports on the radio network: not anywhere in Asia but in North Platte, Nebraska. Two days later, we reached Sioux City to spend a few days before heading back to Bangkok.

Upon my wife's and my return, Jim Coyne said that the Afghan mujahedeen had captured two Soviet soldiers inside Afghanistan and were holding them in Peshawar, Pakistan. CBS in New York agreed for our crew to fly to Pakistan to interview the Soviet captives.

We were met in Peshawar by a small group of Mujahideen who led us to their safe house, a ubiquitous concrete structure among other houses inside a walled compound. After a few minutes, the hosts brought out the two prisoners and ordered both to sit on benches in the courtyard.

They were physically quite different and reportedly had different assignments in the Soviet Army. The younger man was Igor Raikov, a gangly and anxious conscript with Slavic looks. He said he was a simple truck driver and that he was very homesick. His captors did not correct any of his statements, an indication that their interrogation methods had assured them that there was little attempted deception and intelligence value on his part.

The second prisoner was dramatically different. His name was Klaime ("KLI-mee") Lefshuvulovich; his swarthy features were Georgian, not Slavic. He was shorter, had darker skin, and was more muscular than Raikov. Although he did not volunteer information, his captors said that he had admitted during his interrogation(s) that he was Soviet Spetsnaz, or Special Forces. He may have parachuted into Kabul in 1979 as the first wave of the invasion. His body language and threatening glares during our interviews seemed to confirm his apparent Spetsnaz designation.

Our interviews lasted until lunchtime. We returned to our hotel to prepare for the return flight to Bangkok. We learned nothing more about the fate of either Russian soldier. We surmised that they were probably executed once the Mujahideen determined neither one had any more usefulness.

My wife became pregnant in the spring. She gave birth in early November to our son Donald Marvin Hatcher, nicknamed Donnie. He was born at an excellent private hospital in Bangkok. The total fees for delivery and maternity ward care were incredibly inexpensive.

His birth had a minor complication: some of his new skin had attached itself to Vasana's skin inside the womb. The problem was corrected without any lasting effects. Vanessa's birth two years later would have more serious birth defects, as is detailed later.

Donnie was christened informally a few weeks later by Father Joe Maier, an American Roman Catholic priest. He led parishioners in Laos before relocating to Bangkok. His local fame arose from his ministry among the lower class residents in the sprawling slums of the neighborhood of Klong Toei. Fathers supported their families mostly by working in the slaughterhouse nearby or as stevedores at the port of Bangkok, also nearby.

Father Maier lived in a small apartment above the slaughterhouse, his claim to fame among may expats regardless of religion. Neither Vasana nor I assigned religious significance to the christening other than a celebration of a healthy new baby. Donnie and his young sister were baptized as Christians once our family relocated to the US.

Another famous personality shared a bittersweet meeting with Donnie a few weeks later. Walter and Betsy Cronkite were visiting former professional acquaintances in Bangkok. They invited us to bring Donnie for their blessing one evening at the Oriental Hotel. Donnie was doing fine in Walter's arms while all of us were in a breezeway. A sudden bit of thunder and rain squall scared him, however, to the point of our son peeing on Walter Cronkite!

We joked that the accident confirmed Walter's customary signoff ending every evening newscast in the US: "And that's the way it is!"

Walter Cronkite blesses our newborn son Donnie.

Betsy and Walter Cronkite with Derek Williams, Brian Ellis, and Hatcher.

\#   \#   \#

CHAPTER 21

Going to India Twice in Five Months on the Same Story with an Unhappy Ending

THE NEW YEAR of 1984 began with the three of us flying to the US to show Donnie off to our family. CBS News also asked me to come back to New York for two days to meet new people on the Foreign Desk and working for both radio and television. The network was kind enough to pay for Vasana to fly to New York with Donnie for the visit. That allowed a short reunion with Vasana's cousin in New York City.

CBS wanted me to return to Taiwan on assignment. The PRC was rattling sabers over the contentious US-Taiwan relationship under the Taiwan Relations Act. One of the background interviews I conducted was with the *de facto* US ambassador in Taipei, James Lilley, whose official title was Director of the American Institute on Taiwan.

Lilley was a fascinating study among American foreign service officers. He was born in China in 1928, twenty years before the Maoist takeover. His father was employed by Standard Oil, and his mother was a teacher. His Chinese *amah*, a live-in babysitter, taught him to read and speak the Mandarin language fluently.

Lilley's original employment in government was with the CIA, with a series of assignments in Laos, Japan, Hong Kong, Taiwan, and mainland China.

Lilley's skill in reading Mandarin was such that he read Chinese newspapers quite easily—a feat he demonstrated for my benefit, when he read off front-page headlines of several Chinese-language newspapers on his office coffee table. After that assignment in Taipei, he became ambassador to South Korea, among other diplomatic positions.

A few weeks after my return from Taipei, the Indian government admitted that its patience had worn out trying to negotiate with armed Sikh militants in that religion's holiest site, the Golden Temple in Amritsar. Amritsar was close to the contested border with Pakistan and adjacent to the Indian region of Jammu. The tourist destination of Kashmir and its many lakes was also nearby.

Indian Prime Minister Indira Gandhi authorized Operation Blue Star to attack the Golden Temple and other Sikh temples around Amritsar, where armed Sikh militants kept up attacks demanding secession or autonomy in a new country to be called Khalistan.

Amritsar was close to the Pakistan border. India's Cold War ally, The Soviet Union, charged that Pakistan and the US CIA were fomenting the unrest. No proof existed, but PM Gandhi was determined to end the continuing guerilla war. On June 3 Indian Army units, including a division-sized unit and several police and parachute reinforcements, launched a massive attack on the greatly outnumbered Sikh militants inside the Golden Temple. Losses were extremely high on both sides, including among civilians who were to take refuge in the temples or were trapped once the massive battle began.

CBS dispatched our crew to New Delhi. We arrived and explored ways to get closest to the site of the bloodshed. The Indian government had put the entire region off-limits to foreigners and civilians of all types. We took an hourlong domestic flight to Jammu City, but that was still three hours by roads that were lined with numerous blockades and checkpoints.

We returned to New Delhi empty-handed. But we did succeed in getting an interview with PM Gandhi, plus an interview with India's famous Sikh author, Kushwant Singh. Singh was famous for his historical novel *Train to Pakistan* in 1956 about the chaotic ethnic movements resulting from the hasty UK effort to grant Indian and Pakistani independence.

We were able to satellite a story to New York featuring on-camera comments by both personalities, Singh and Mrs. Gandhi. As we learned, Singh presented an alternative view that infuriated the prime minister.

We waited in New Delhi for new developments and requested another interview with Mrs. Gandhi. Her press relations assistant quickly and decisively turned us down, a sign of Mrs. Gandhi's furious reaction to our story.

Five months later, two of her Sikh bodyguards assassinated her in the garden of her official residence. She was cornered on her way to an interview by the late British actor Peter Ustinov. Why she had kept Sikh bodyguards in her employ was a question being asked all over the globe. One assassin had been on her staff for only five months; the second guard was removed after the battle at the Golden Temple, only to be reinstated on her command.

Television crews and others from around the world covered the aftermath and the funeral. Numerous heads of state and international celebrities like Ustinov attended the cremation near the Raj Ghat, a memorial complex dedicated to Mahatma Gandhi. (Despite having the same last name, Indira was the daughter of the other giant in India's struggle for independence, Jawaharlal Nehru.)

The following countries sent their prime ministers or presidents to the sad occasion: Australia, the Czech Republic, Japan, Laos, Fiji, France, New Zealand, Cambodia, Poland, Uganda, United Kingdom, and Vietnam.

Secretary of State George Schultz represented the US.

The Philippines' First Lady Imelda Marcos represented her husband, Ferdinand. Her older daughter Imee Marcos was among the official delegation. (My amusing personal interaction with Imee on the flight from New Delhi to Bangkok follows.)

CBS big-footed two of us Asia-based reporters by sending in big-name London correspondent, Steve Kroft. Kroft would win an Emmy for his reporting on Mrs. Gandhi's funeral. I was fortunate enough before the actual cremation to interview Ustinov for CBS radio and television.

The most memorable event of that entire trip occurred as I settled into my first-class seat enroute back to Bangkok. A large number of impressive people paraded onto the aircraft, leading the way for Imee Marcos, who gracefully lowered herself into the very next seat!

She was every bit as attractive in person as she was in contemporary photos. Before departure, a cabin attendant came to take our drink preferences. I asked Imee to name the drink of her choice. She smiled and said, "How about champagne?" No argument there. Either champagne or mimosas, a very civilized way to fly.

Wherever her retinue of assistants were sitting, no one bothered her until just before the landing in Bangkok. We disembarked to find the Philippines ambassador waiting.

The ambassador was none other than a dear friend of mine and fellow West Point graduate, retired Philippine Army general Rafael "Rocky" Ileto, USMA class of 1943. As a Philippine Army officer serving first in World War II, then in successive senior positions in the Philippine Armed Forces, he led a storied and heroic career.

He and I met for the first time in Pittsburgh in 1969 when he was among twenty-five foreign generals and admirals attending a three-week professional management seminar sponsored by the US Department of Defense. I was one of the three junior officers serving as temporary aides to the foreign officers.

His assignment to Bangkok in 1980 as his country's ambassador allowed me to renew acquaintances. We saw each other every year thereafter at the annual West Point Founders' Day Dinners.

Back to Imee Marcos and Ambassador Ileto. He was under orders to ensure her smooth transfer to the flight to Manila. His face broke into a broad grin when the aircraft door opened and out stepped yours truly, ever the West Point gentleman, leading the First Family's daughter and retinue off the aircraft! She was surprised to learn that her country's ambassador and I were longtime friends.

I said my goodbyes to both, never to see either in person again. Rocky Ileto passed away in 2003 of a heart attack. He was buried with full military honors, a great soldier and diplomat. Imee Marcos has become involved in Filipino politics, no surprise. As of this writing, she is a senator. She and her brother are continuing the Marcos legacy. That brother, Ferdinand "Bong-bong" Marcos, is the president of the Philippines at this writing.

CHAPTER 22

My Last Few Days with CBS News and My Farewell to Thailand, December 1984

As THE YEAR wound to a close, and with the reelection in the US of President Reagan, I had become anxious about the next steps in my irregular career pattern. I began to have self-doubt that I seemed to have lost some favor in the eyes of CBS bosses in New York. In earlier years, my superiors in Hong Kong, Tokyo, and New York had occasionally stressed the need to hold serious talks about my future. Events in Asia, and foreign news in general however, always seemed to be moving too fast to have those negotiations occur. I considered talking to a talent agent in New York to increase my leverage, not just with CBS but with the other two major networks.

I turned away overtures to sign on with NBC News, despite pleas from its Asia bureau chief in Tokyo. I admired almost all the folks I knew in the CBS galaxy. I felt loyal to CBS, perhaps more than I should have.

Another serious decision concerned our one-year-old son's early childhood education, along with younger siblings who might follow him. If CBS failed to offer me a more permanent contract, and if there was no follow-through by NBC, I worried that continuing my year-on-year status without an *expatriate employment package* (including education tuition) might force me to absorb prohibitive international school tuition costs that were usually covered by the American networks for staff employees.

Son Donnie with dad, 2012.

Within a few days of President Reagan's victory, I received an encouraging letter from Richard Armitage, my close American friend with whom I first crossed paths in 1977. He had returned shortly thereafter to Washington and assumed positions first as a senior aide to US Senator Bob Dole and later in the Department of Defense managing political-military relationships with many Asian countries. Shortly before the 1984 presidential campaign, Rich assumed fuller duties managing such relationships beyond Asia in Latin America, the Middle East, and Africa.

I was fortunate enough to sustain our friendship after our short time together in Bangkok. Rich was well-known throughout the American foreign policy community in 1975 when he led the last flotilla of Vietnamese Navy ships out of Saigon to marry up with US Navy ships in the South China Sea.

He wrote in his warm note to me that there would be personnel changes in Washington during Reagan's second term, and he would consider having me come to work for him as one of his regional advisors.

I decided to take that bold step and return to the US and go to work for Rich in the Defense Department. I made no real attempt to seek wise counsel from others, e.g., my parents, my wife, or other closest friends with my best interests at heart. I turned in short and respectful letters of resignation to all three key clients: CBS News, BBC, and *Newsweek*.

Vasana and I packed out and transported our household goods to the US. We sold our Volvo 244DL sedan, famous from its role in our courtship. Our last couple of days in a five-star hotel were bittersweet. We were leaving my wife's country of birth, I was relinquishing the exciting occupation and frequent travel that I had enjoyed for the last eight years.

#   #   #

CHAPTER 23

In the US with A New Family and A Brand-New Set of Circumstances, 1985–1988

"Because of the Lord's great love, we are not
consumed, for His compassions never fail. They are
new every morning, great is your faithfulness"

—Lam. 3:22–23, NIV.

AFTER SPENDING TWELVE of my last fourteen years in Asia, I returned to the US with my lovely new wife and one-year-old Donnie. We spent the Christmas holidays in Sioux City with my parents, who were ecstatic at spoiling grandson Donald Marvin (named for his grandfather and great-grandfather).

I began to understand the sadness felt by either set of grandparents when grandchildren like Donnie were far from one of the two pairs. In our case, Vasana's parents had to say goodbye to Donnie and their daughter, turning the three of us over to Donnie's American grandparents half a world away.

Vasana accepted her fate with fortitude and optimism. I realized she would be very sad to leave her parents. I kept telling myself that moving my family to almost any major population center in the US other than the Washington, DC, area would mean severe homesickness. She would be without any close former acquaintances of any type from Thailand, except her cousin in New York, my parents in Iowa, or her sisters-in-law in Denver and the Twin Cities.

The new way of life in the Virginia suburbs was not completely dismal. She renewed friendships with mutual friends from Bangkok who preceded us and were now living in or near the nation's capital, whether those friends were Thai, Vietnamese, American, or other nationalities.

In almost all ways, the major relocation would unleash significant changes to our lifestyles as a young couple with one-year-old Donnie.

For Donnie, he no longer had close proximity to his maternal grand-parents and the attention from a full-time maid.

For Vasana, the relocation allowed informal reunions with some familiar faces, when virtually everything else was another test of culture shock: no longer having any domestic help as before, and with her in-laws (my parents) hundreds of miles away in Iowa rather than her parents being just a half hour away in Bangkok. Learning to shop for groceries, clothing, and other necessities of a young family, especially for her son and herself. She learned to drive in a new country where everyone drove on the other side of the road from Thailand. Her beginning fluency in English was only that—beginning.

She was fortunate when it came to grocery shopping, not because of nearby American grocery chains but because of the numerous small Asian and international grocery stores around Falls Church, Arlington, and other suburbs. Within a few years, some of the large American food chains started introducing a larger and larger variety of Asian vegetables and herbs, among other items, in their produce sections.

Homesickness was often close at hand. One small antidote to that was an unusual telephonic connection in Bangkok. A friend there was an international telephone operator. Somehow, he was able to "game the system" at no cost to her by connecting her calls to her parents. Overseas calls at the time could run as high as fifteen dollars for three minutes. That was the price I paid in Bangkok for infrequent calls to my parents or other friends.

And for me, it was a very great change in professional obligations, responsibilities, and working conditions. The several years stationed overseas with a high-pressure American news network involved working with relatively few professional equals and having easy access to a small hierarchy of news producers, bureau chiefs, and managers. Now a Pentagon civil servant and in an environment full of pressure, I was among many well-educated government civil servants, military staff officers, and other colleagues, in a much more rigid federal government hierarchy. There was also the comparison between the daily lifestyle in Asia of frequent travel combined with very busy or less busy days as an overseas reporter, compared to a much more regimented, professional hierarchy and office environment.

My official appointment as a foreign affairs staff officer also meant that 70 to 80 percent of workload involved handling classified information and communications.

Another big difference was our changed financial situation. During the last few years with CBS, I worked on a salaried contract that was very sufficient, given our very few significant financial obligations. Those included a relatively small monthly rental for our two-bedroom house, gasoline and maintenance for the recent-model Volvo sedan we already owned, very few medical expenses and medicines, and considerable discretionary income. The earnings from assignments for the BBC and *Newsweek* were additional income.

A footnote on income: The IRS allows a "foreign-earned income exclusion" that excludes a certain amount of income from taxation for American citizens residing overseas or who are out of the country eleven months of any calendar year. In the years in Thailand, I either never earned enough (in the first couple of years) to even file a tax return, or in later years I did not pay income tax because my taxable income from US sources did not exceed the plateau (then $75,000). Any exclusion of such a healthy amount would have meant greatly increased discretionary income, of course.

Upon arrival in the US, we stayed with close friends from Thailand, Mike and Chan Eiland, for several days while house-hunting. Mike was a West Point graduate in the class of 1961, seven years my senior. We overlapped a decade earlier in military assignments in Thailand, to include membership in and parachute jumping with the Mitrapab Educational Foundation. His lovely Vietnamese wife, Chan, also traveled with us and participated in demonstrations. Both of them have remained dear friends for half a century.

Mike Eiland.

We were able to make a sizeable down payment on a new three-bedroom house in Falls Church. My first mortgage came with an interest rate of 13 percent. Thirteen percent!

Fortunately, I was able to refinance the mortgage a year and a half later down to a 6.5 percent interest rate resulting in a much smaller monthly obligation. I obviously had more bills, such as car payments, family medical visits, home and automobile insurance, cable television, and utilities. Within a year, we had our second child, accompanied by enormous neonatal expenses for a premature birth with complications. I had no health insurance at the time. Our lifestyle was a bit cramped.

Starting such a new chapter would lead to my first midlife crisis, complicated by the birth of a second child and other new routines.

I tried to keep some familiar routines. I continued my jogging nearly every day, either on the new city streets near our new home or during lunchtime near the Pentagon. On many weekends, I competed informally in a variety of organized races I remembered a quote from James Fixx's best-selling book on running: "To run is to live. Everything else is just waiting." (After two best-selling books on the subject, he passed away in a sad irony at the age of 52.)

The Friday edition of the *Washington Post* always listed a variety of weekend races. It was easy to run races of different distances from five kilometers to ten miles and even up to a half marathon somewhere nearby.

That first year I finished the Marine Corps Marathon in three and a half hours. Two years later, I would get to cut about ten minutes off that time.

I realized how long that first marathon was the very next day. I ached from the muscle tears on my quadriceps from the three hours of exertion. For the next few days, I went down any flights of stairs backwards because of the extreme soreness in my quads. Working in the Pentagon on both occasions, one could always note those brand-new marathoners by observing men and women descending the stairways backwards.

While in Thailand I collected running shoes almost as an afterthought: popular brands such as Nike, Puma, and Reebok as well as lesser-known labels including Brooks, Saucony, and Asics. I compared running the first time in a pair of well-cushioned Brooks shoes, to running on pillows. The extreme comfort was proof of the nonstop competitive engineering by companies making running shoes.

My fulltime position at the Pentagon entitled me to membership in the Pentagon Officers' Athletic Club (POAC), where I could enjoy all the below-ground facilities near a main entrance: secure locker space, showers, weight rooms, downsized basketball courts, lap pools for swimming, and handball and squash courts.

The annual cost for POAC membership was $110, a great bargain. At lunchtime every day, in all seasons, great numbers of office workers would don their running gear and leave the Pentagon for the paths nearby, crossing Memorial Bridge into DC to continue jogging either around the National Mall or along the DC side down to Hains Point and back.

Based on my previous six years on active duty, I was reinstated in the US Army Reserves, even despite the several years' absence living in Thailand. Among other accomplishments was my 1989 diploma from the US Army Command and General Staff Course, most of which I took by correspondence.

But the greatest memory of that time in the army reserves was a two-week temporary duty assignment at the Sixth US Army Headquarters at the Presidio in San Francisco in 1985. An army officer friend since military intelligence school at Fort Huachuca arranged for me to give two classified terrorism briefings to a group of officers in the Sixth Army jurisdiction.

While at the Presidio, I thoroughly enjoyed my daily runs, especially two on perfect Bay Area autumn afternoons. I treasured both times running across the Golden Gate Bridge and back, absorbing pleasing visual and auditory stimuli the entire way. I am reminded of those runs anytime I see a picture of the iconic bridge.

The rest of 1985 became a whirlwind of activity, including almost immediate travel from Washington to New York City on official business. The whirlwind would be capped off by another around-the-world trip from Washington. The stops for business included Bahrain and Pakistan. A third stop was in Bangkok to pick up my young family. We returned to Washington via Tokyo and New York's JFK Airport.

The earlier trip to New York was to manage a semi-classified breakfast meeting at the famous Waldorf Astoria Hotel between Secretary of Defense Caspar Weinberger and the Thai prime minister, retired Thai Army General Prem Tinsulanonda, to sign a joint agreement continuing US military access to an ammunition storage facility for regional contingencies. Among all the senior officers and Secretary Weinberger, I was the boy Friday for all organizational details. Fortunately, all went well.

One irony of that meeting was my greeting the Thai prime minister (already in New York for the annual United Nations General Assembly sessions). Just a couple of years earlier, I sat at the head table for a formal banquet in Bangkok, hosting the same Thai prime minister in my role as President of the Foreign Correspondents' Club of Thailand. In New York, the Thai Prime Minister might have wondered about my unusual transition from foreign correspondent days in Bangkok to a staff officer in the Pentagon.

A few days later, in a sideways move from being the action officer handling political-military affairs for countries in Southeast Asia, Rich Armitage asked me to assume similar duties for Pakistan, Afghanistan, and Bangladesh, with backup responsibilities for India and smaller countries in south Asia.

As an abrupt introduction to those duties, I was included on a special military manifest to fly to Islamabad with senior officials for the semiannual defense cooperation meetings with Pakistan. We made an overnight stop in Bahrain for discussions with the American ambassador there and his embassy staff.

The three days of official meetings in Pakistan before assuming duties in Washington afforded me the opportunity just to sit and listen. Almost all aspects of the very difficult and sensitive relationship were discussed, including the situation in Afghanistan and negotiations over supplying specific military items for Pakistan's defenses. Pakistan was an original signatory to SEATO (Southeast Asia Treaty Organization), i.e., an ally since 1954, under the American government policy of containment of Communist regimes, especially those in Moscow, Beijing, and Communist satellites from eastern Europe to Asia.

One of the three days was reserved for a field observation trip to the border defenses in and around Peshawar, including a helicopter visit with Pakistani escorts to the famous Khyber Pass between Pakistan and Afghanistan. Our lunch that day was in the formal officers' mess of the prestigious unit known as the Khyber Rifles—one of the eight paramilitary units the British Army recruited and formed in the late nineteenth century, composed of tribesmen from the Northwest Frontier. Their primary mission from then until modern times was the defense of the Khyber Pass. The excellent luncheon was followed by a traditional concert involving bagpipes and other martial musical instruments.

Those semiannual meetings took on far more significance within a few months. In March 1986, Soviet-supplied fighter bombers launched cross-border bombing attacks into Pakistan, targeting Afghan refugee camps and villages around Peshawar and causing major casualties. The Soviet-backed attack was thought to have been a warning signal to Pakistan not to proceed with acquiring sophisticated American early warning aircraft, either AWACS or US Navy E-2C aircraft.

After the conclusion in Islamabad of the joint meetings and my observer's role, I flew to Bangkok to pick up my wife and son, Donnie. They had flown to Bangkok a month earlier to spend time with Vasana's family. Vasana's mother quickly perceived that Vasana was pregnant with our next child. I spent a few days with the family and seeing former Bangkok friends before putting all four of us (counting our embryonic daughter) on the trans-Pacific flights to Washington.

Back in the small Pentagon office I shared with the other colleague managing South Asian affairs, Mark Palevitz, and with my new countries of responsibility, I began soaking up and contributing to policy changes in the sensitive relationships among Pakistan, India, and the Soviet-backed government in Afghanistan. I worked daily with field-grade military officers and DOD civilian employees answering to their superiors on the Joint

Staff and in the Defense Security Assistance Agency, plus counterparts in the Department of State, the DIA, and the CIA. Several of these men and women were profiled in George Crile's classic book *Charlie Wilson's War*.

For the next few months, my attention was divided between professional duties and the home front, with the time drawing near for Vasana's delivery of our second child. That birth and care would be far more difficult for us than caring for Donnie two and a half years before.

The difficulties began five weeks before the expected delivery date. Vasana's water broke one morning in early February while I was in the Pentagon office. She notified me and called a girlfriend, who rushed Vasana to Shady Grove Adventist Hospital in Silver Spring, Maryland.

Vasana contacted another close Thai friend to take Donnie to their home. Once I knew that Donnie was safe, I drove to the hospital. At the time of Vanessa's delivery, the state of Maryland allowed husbands to be inside the operating room. I was ushered into the Operating Room a few minutes before the actual delivery.

No one—not Vasana, the Thai doctor, or I—was prepared for the physical problems our daughter would experience from her premature birth on February 12, the birthdate of another great American, former president Abraham Lincoln.

Dad and Vanessa, 2012.

What was immediately noticeable to all of us in the Operating Room was the tiny girl's misshapen nose. It was an irregular square of soft flesh with a jagged crease from top to bottom. Another anomaly was what seemed to be a wider-than-normal separation between Vanessa's eye sockets.

The obstetrician suggested I return home and wait for word overnight about the conditions of both mother and daughter. I drove back to pick up Donnie and head back home.

Later that night the doctor called to say that he and other doctors had decided to transfer Vanessa to the ICU ward at Children's Hospital in Washington, given not only the *facial dysplasia* at birth but other signs of abnormality. Vasana would recuperate at Shady Grove Adventist for a day or two.

The next day I called my parents to describe the situation. I begged them to consider coming to help me tend to Donnie and care for Vasana and our brand-new, premature daughter. My parents flew to Washington the very next day. Vasana and I are forever grateful for their willingness to show up. Years later I was reminded of their love by a friend's statement, "You can fake caring, but you can't fake showing up." My parents' example of Christian tenderness and compassion, and familial love for their son, daughter-in-law, and two young grandchildren, helped speed a life-changing spiritual change in me.

The next several days were a maelstrom of activity and deep concern over the lives of mother and child. Vasana suffered postpartum depression after her discharge. She languished briefly at home before agreeing to see her new daughter in the ICU ward for premature babies.

Mercifully, my parents were indispensable in handling all sorts of tasks. I tried to maintain my professional duties and do what I could in helping Vasana readjust to regular household duties, as we all dealt with the range of emotions over a troubled premature delivery of a new little girl with a handful of neonatal challenges. I also needed to to help Donnie cope with new realities.

The five of us, my parents, Vasana, Donnie and I made several journeys over the next ten days to Children's Hospital. Vasana began to shower love on her tiny daughter who was facing indetermined long-term effects, possibly including some degree of mental retardation.

Vanessa lay in her crib at the ICU among numerous other "preemies", many with medical problems far more challenging than hers.

One of the most poignant memories came on the first few days at the ICU. Siblings of any of those in the ICU ward were prevented from entering the ward proper. Donnie would stand at the doorway to the ward and peer inside. He had no guarantee that he would be able to catch a glimpse of his new sister, much less figure out what was really going on. His bond and his concern would translate in later years to great affection and heart-to-heart compassion for Vanessa, with God's blessings.

The fantastic pediatric specialists at Children's Hospital started to consult with us about the handful of problems facing Vanessa. The first issue was the nature of her misshapen nose with the nasty crease. Doctors advised us that during development of the fetus in the womb, the middle of the face is one of the last areas to fully form. Plates of skin and soft tissue come together from both sides of the head. The misshapen nose was the product of some slight anomaly during that very late stage of fetal development. The doctors advised that she would be a candidate for plastic surgery in a few years.

The second issue with her face was the slightly wider-than-normal separation of her eye sockets. The specialists were worried about the possibility of serious vision problems: the eyes may not see in parallel, leading to undetermined problems of perception.

The specialists advised reevaluation frequently for the next few months. If surgery was absolutely required, the surgeons would have to break the bones of each socket and move the sockets slightly closer together before mending the bone structures. That sounded like terrifying surgery. Fortunately, the doctors concluded after weeks of observation that her vision seemed normal. A major relief for us and for Vanessa.

She also exhibited heart arrhythmia, given her premature birth. We equipped the crib in our bedroom with a heart monitor to signal any trouble breathing. Again, we were fortunate that no serious issues ever occurred, thanks be to God.

Lastly, the doctors tried as gently as possible to tell us that, given the totality of the conditions and the premature nature of birth, there was some chance of long-term cognitive disability.

Hardly encouraging news, to be sure.

Another strain on the entire affair was the enormous financial burden I would bear. At the Pentagon I was not officially a federal employee, meaning that I was not eligible for health insurance coverage afforded full time employees. I faced a debt of more than $14,000 for the hospital birth and immediate ICU care at Children's Hospital. I was able to pay most of those costs, but the family had to forego a great deal of discretionary income for more than a year.

I would not realize God's great dollops of grace and mercy, when I deserved neither, until a couple of years later when my first midlife crisis brought this prodigal to his knees. I experienced two decades of spiritual darkness since my leaving home for West Point. Only a few years later would I take to heart the admonition in 1 John 1:9—"If we confess our sins, God is faithful and just to forgive us our sins and cleanse us of all unrighteousness." And the wonderful quote from Soren Kirkegaard: "Life must be lived forwards but can only be understood backwards."

Once Vanessa was released from Children's Hospital, I did not endear myself to my older sister, Carole, and her husband, Roger, nor to my parents, because of my confusion and arrogance. Aunt Carole had sent clothing outfits as gifts for Vanessa. During all the stress of the entire ordeal, I did not thank Carole in any way for her loving thoughtfulness. I was the classic ingrate, entirely and solely at fault. My mother called to read me the riot act, deservedly. I meekly called Carole to apologize to the greatest extent and admit my total responsibility. Despite my best efforts, the others involved probably labeled my gesture as "too little, too late." To this day, I am ashamed of my grievous oversight and behavior.

Our family worked through a series of medical appointments given all the abnormalities described here. Just by sheer determination to take all of the issues one day at a time were we able to maintain a fragile hold on normalcy. More of God's prevenient grace.

Within a year, however, many of the difficulties were overcome through the obvious toughness and strong will of our little daughter. It would be another couple of years, however, before the chief plastic surgeon at Children's Hospital felt the time was right to reshape Vanessa's nose.

The issue of potential retardation started to fade after a visit to the facility for Fairfax County families, where early childhood professionals examined toddlers for signs of retardation. The specialists felt confident that their tests revealed that Vanessa had overcome the mix of physical imperfections and would suffer no long-term retardation. Thanks be to God. Rinse and repeat.

A few years later, as she was turning five years old, her plastic surgery would prove successful. The relief for Vasana especially, and the spectacular self-esteem and self-confidence Vanessa gained from her much more normal appearance, meant everything to us. Such self-confidence and self-esteem, forming a unique blend of charm, charisma, and confidence, caused her American grandmother to jokingly remark one day, "You're going to have trouble with that one!"

Her grandmother was so prescient. In a way, Vanessa would rule the world. And she does. Our world. Within a few years, she would spread her wings and fly, first in preschool ballet lessons and piano lessons. At Hillsdale College, she majored in rhetoric and communications *cum laude* and took minors in vocal performance and piano performance.

A perfect example of her charm and self-confidence came when she was seven years old, during a family vacation, with grandparents, aunts, uncles, cousins, and Mom and Dad and Donnie. She had been taking piano lessons for only a year or so, but with little stage fright, she decided to entertain at dinner one evening at a lake resort in Minnesota. She strode over to the communal piano and, to the delight of everyone in the dining room, threw herself into a virtually perfect piano rendition—without sheet music—of *Rockin' Rhythm.*

Vanessa's graduation from Hillsdale College, 2008.

Slightly forgotten in all of Vanessa's medical issues was her older brother. Vanessa showed her admiration for him in a preschool ballet performance. Donnie, Mom, and Dad had seats close to the stage, and in an ad lib moment, Vanessa looked out into the audience, caught Donnie's eye, waved at him, and shouted, "Hi, Donnie!" Not any word of recognition for her mom and dad, but a younger sister's infatuation with an older brother. Very sweet.

Donnie had his own serious medical challenges a few years later. He was diagnosed with scoliosis that would require many hours of complicated surgery to open his back and attach metal rods to straighten his spine. As the preliminary to the full surgery, the surgeons sliced into his side and shaved off fragments of bone from his rib cage. The fragments covered the metal rods and would graft onto the spine over time.

That surgery was performed at Children's Hospital when Donnie turned fourteen. He was heavily sedated throughout the nearly fourteen-hour surgery. When he awoke from the anesthesia, he told Vasana that it didn't last very long at all! A great endorsement for the abilities of the doctors, especially the anesthesiologist. More of God's grace for our family.

Donnie was strongly advised not to engage in any contact sports and had to give up skateboarding, to avoid collisions or falls that might cause damage to the spine and to the metal rods. That surgery and related medical charges would be completely covered by health insurance provided by my employer then, an energy development firm managed by a West Point classmate of mine, as described in a later chapter.

CHAPTER 24

The Repentance of a Penitent Prodigal Son, 1988–1990

"For the message of the cross is foolishness to
those who are perishing, but to those of us who
are being saved, it is the power of God"

—1 Cor. 1:18, NIV.

"For it is by grace that you have been saved, through
faith—and this is not from yourselves, but from
God—not by works, so that no one can boast"

—Eph. 2:8–9, NIV.

"Here is a trustworthy saying that deserves full
acceptance: Christ Jesus came into the world
to save sinner—of who I am the worst"

—1 Tim. 1:15, NIV.

SON OF THE HEARTLAND

"Train up a child in the way he should go, and
when he is old, he will not depart from it."

—Proverbs 22:6, KJV.

THE BIGGEST TURNAROUND in my decision in 1988 to leave the somewhat prestigious job in the Pentagon working on political-military relationships was my transformation from the prodigal lifestyle until then: similar to, but not quite as absolute as, that described in the parable of the prodigal son in Luke 15.

Actually, the radical change was due to the Humble Hound of Heaven, but radical change it was, thanks to a "stabbed-in-the-heart" reaction to a powerful sermon that year.

I had signed up for two consecutive personal growth weekends that summer led by a group called Lifespring. Mentors challenged all participants with two questions: "What are you pretending not to know?" and "What kind of legacy are you creating and leaving behind for your offspring?"

My overt response to both questions quickly followed, thanks to the Holy Spirit. I realized that my adult years in the military and then as a foreign reporter in Asia resembled some of the prodigal nature of that character in Luke 15.

My first step was to change the destiny of our very young children. I put them into a weekly Sunday school routine for their own, and our family's, benefit.

My lovely wife had been forced to fly back to Thailand that summer. Her mother had been hospitalized after a traffic accident in Bangkok. Adoring and worried daughter spent more than a month caring for ailing mother. Fortunately, there was no lasting damage.

In her absence and on a brisk Sunday in September, I piled Donnie (aged four and a half) and Vanessa (aged two and a half) into the car and drove the half mile to the closest United Methodist church. I grew up in a midsize Methodist church in Iowa. The three of us sat near the rear of the sanctuary. We knew no one in attendance—not the preacher, other celebrants, or congregants.

The Scripture passage that morning was the powerful story from the prophet Isaiah in chapter six of that book:

> In the year that King Uzziah died, I saw the Lord, high and exalted, seated on a throne; and the train of his robe filled the temple. [2] Above him were seraphim, each with six wings: With two wings they covered their faces, with two they covered their feet, and with two they were flying. [3] And they were calling to one another: "Holy, holy, holy is the LORD Almighty; the whole earth is full of his glory." [4] At the sound of their voices the doorposts and thresholds shook, and the temple was filled with smoke. [5]"Woe to me!" I cried. "I am ruined! For I am a man of unclean lips, and I live among a people of unclean lips, and my eyes have seen the King, the LORD Almighty." [6] Then one of the seraphim flew to me with a live coal in his hand, which he had taken with tongs from the altar. [7] With it he touched my mouth and said, "See, this has touched your lips; your guilt is taken away and your sin atoned for." Then I heard the voice of the Lord saying, "Whom shall I send? And who will go for us?" And I said, "Here am I. Send me!"

"Here am I. Send me." Bang! Talk about a rallying "Win one for the Gipper" cry! This in the middle of my midlife crisis now becoming a pivotal moment heading into my middle age.

Attending a mainstream Protestant worship service after many years away from the Lord—except for times with parents when I was back from Thailand or Christmas Eve services at local churches in Virginia (not Easter services, oddly enough)—was inspirational beyond Isaiah's response "Here am I. Send me." Similar to the famous quote from *The Karate Kid*: "When the student is ready, the teacher will appear."

That Sunday morning, while Vasana was in Thailand caring for her mother, was the first of repeat attendances the next few Sundays. We were visited one evening by Pastor Charles Blalock and a lay member, Craig Day. Pastor Blalock and his wife, Jesse, were transferred elsewhere in Virginia within a few short years, and I lost track of them.

Craig became my first link to Graham Road United Methodist Church—and very much remains a strong Christian brother (and a now-retired US Defense Department civilian employee).

From left to right: Cliff Mauck, Hatcher, and Craig
Day—Promise Keepers rally, 1997.

Later that fall I asked my parents to request the transfer of my long-dormant membership from the church in Iowa. Our young family became regular attendees—but without my wife's conversion from the dominant religion of Thailand: Buddhism.

My decisions to reengage in a local Protestant church and to enroll both children in Sunday school included my joining the small church choir and attending the monthly men's breakfasts, inter alia. I became friends with many church members, to my family's benefit.

I volunteered before one Saturday morning breakfast to give a short speech on the very interesting history of the city of Falls Church (the same speech I'd given earlier at my local Toastmasters club). Briefly and without any other details of the city's role in the Revolutionary War and the Civil War, I highlighted the history and geography of the first settlement and the construction and naming of the Falls Church—reprised briefly here.

On one voyage up the Potomac River in the early seventeenth century, Captain John Smith and party were unable to traverse the dangerous falls in the river at what is now Great Falls. When disembarking, they followed a group of Native Americans on a small trail from the river, where they had been fishing, to a much larger trail. That trail was a well-used migration route Native Americans used from the Tidewater area out to the Shenandoah Mountains.

The intersection of those trails would become the main intersection of modern-day Falls Church. The migration trail became Highway 7/Leesburg Pike, and the trail from the Potomac River to the larger trail became roughly Little Falls Street through what is now North Arlington and the northeastern part of Falls Church.

The actual Church by the Falls, i.e., the Falls Church, was built just off the intersection and originally served members of the vestry including George Washington and George Mason.

This is the end of the brief history of the town and the church after which it was named.

Back to the early 1990s: our family was befriended at our new church, and my wife was able to enjoy new friendships with several couples, who quickly grew to love her and our two children. This was before Vanessa's first plastic surgery to correct her disfigured nose from her 1986 birth.

One of the new habits I began to nurture was listening to radio station WFAX AM-1220, Christian Radio for the Nation's Capital, an AM station with 5 kw daytime power just two miles from our home. I began to listen to several preachers in the morning, chief among them Charles Swindoll and his *Insight for Living*, which continues to this day on a number of Christian stations.

Early on, I heard him promote his 1987 book, *Living above the Level of Mediocrity*. I bought the book and started a journal. I still have some of the most powerful passages from the book, including:

"People who soar (above the level of mediocrity) are those who refuse to sit back, sigh, and wish things would change… Rather, they visualize in their minds that they are not quitters; they will not allow life circumstances to push them down and hold then under" (p. 29).

"Those who live, I mean really soar above the grubby, greedy level of mediocrity have learned how to live from the perspective of another kingdom… to give all they have to the Lord God and to trust Him to give back all they need" (p. 47).

"You have to give it ALL away before you can get anything back. People who risk living like that really soar" (p. 47).

"Being different is costly, especially when most are satisfied to blend in… rare are the ones who decide to ignore the 'average' and fight against the pull of the mediocre magnet" (p. 49).

"Deciding to be free, to think and live independently, to soar above the masses is always a costly decision" (p.49).

Another very strong and well-known pastor, the late Charles Stanley, became another fixture in my orbit of solid preachers, through his *In Touch Ministries* radio and television broadcasts. I included a few lists of his from selected sermons in my journal, to which I still refer to this day:

From a sermon "Generous People Are: Happier People; In demand by others; Sensitive to others' desires; Marked by genuine giving; Able to see needs as opportunity, not threat; Question how much to give, not how little; Able to make other who give happy; Able to give by faith; Are other-person oriented; and Know they can't outgive God."

From a sermon "When the Odds Are Against You", Stanley said, "God will use our difficulty to build our faith. God will often require us to do the unreasonable. God will lead us to do what brings Him the most glory. God will strip us of all dependence but Himself. God will encourage the fainthearted. God will always work in the other camp on our behalf. God will give us specific instructions resulting in victory, if we obey".

From a sermon "A Passion to Serve Him": Motivations include "Gratitude for our salvation; Conviction of God's call; Vision for God's purpose; Desire to invest in eternal value; (and) Desire to glorify God."

Stanley listed some requirements: Serve according to God's will, not mine; Serve according to my gifts, not talents; Serve in His power, not human strength; Focus on God, not on the work.

I still listen frequently to both of these powerful preachers, among several others with international ministries and followings.

During the fall of 1990, Pastor Blalock asked me if I would consider giving the sermon for Methodist Laity Sunday. The suggested topic was "Called and Gifted." I agreed and prepared my sermon using the same Scripture passage from Isaiah 6 (among others) to give my perspective on how "Here am I. Send me" fit very well into the general topic of "Called and Gifted."

Excerpts of that sermon follow. The reader may be able to discern how the climactic events of the last few years were leading me to a more dedicated commitment to Christian service. I date calling myself a Christian who admits he is "Unworthy but Forgiven" to those few events two years earlier in the summer of 1988.

I put together my sermon based on the Isaiah Scripture and other references and some thoughts of my own, to wit: "In our own way, we as believers are all called and gifted. In whatever form it may take, believers must continue to answer that call and give of ourselves… There is no gift the universal Christian Church needs that God has not imparted to one or more of its members at a local level. The work of each local church is to encourage the members in the discovery and use of those gifts."

In a later version of the same sermon, I mentioned the wonderful daily devotional book entitled *Abundant Living* by the late E. Stanley Jones, a former missionary in India. In one section, Jones talked about the three faces of Matthew before he became a disciple: the tax collector his friends knew, the inner person that only he himself knew, and the Matthew whom Jesus saw. Each thought he saw the true Matthew.

"Who was right?" I asked the congregation.

> "The Matthew whom Jesus saw was the true Matthew, and so it turned out to be, the Matthew of infinite possibilities, an original disciple, author of one of the four Gospels, and a strong believer. E. Stanley Jones said that about all of us. 'There are three people in each of us: the one your associates see, the outer you; the one you see, the present you; and the one whom Jesus sees, the future you. **Jesus always looks not on what a man or woman has been or is, but on what he or she is going to be.** (Emphasis mine.) Much like the artist who looks not on what the rough piece of stone or empty canvas is, but on what the artist is going to bring out of it: a living sculpture or creative painting.'"

When we respond to that divine wake-up call, I continued, we finally comprehend that Jesus sees the third us, the real personality, being just like other believers: a special child of God in God's eyes, with unique talents and gifts. The gifts God showers upon all of us, like Matthew's Gospel, are for us to give away.

Whitney Houston sang it in a similar way in a single recording, *Didn't We Almost Have It All?* In her words, "Once you know what love is, you never let it end." I continued to think about the comment that Jesus looks not at what a man was or is, but what a man can be. I felt Jesus prodding me to say, "Here am I. Send me." When we see needs in others, we feel called to respond somehow by never letting our giving end.

In that sermon on Laity Sunday back in 1990, I added a personal vignette from my decade in Asia: "Let me recite a few lines written by someone else who is called and gifted: 'We set forth upon one of the few flawless journeys a man can take. To be moving over the desert at night when the great stars are overhead, and a white moon illuminates the ghostly world. A great sweep of desert appearing like a cross between a blizzard of snow and a garden of white flowers in spring, to watch the rise and fall of sand dunes as they make their poetic march across the shadowy horizon... In the distance, a man played a flute, and it was like a scene from *The Arabian Nights.*'"

I went on, "To me, that is incredibly descriptive writing. You can picture yourself taking that journey, the images are so exact. That author: the late James Michener, from his book *Caravans*, about brave nomadic men (long before the Taliban) in Afghanistan.... I have a close friend who can create word pictures just as beautiful and descriptive as Michener's. My friend (another former Asian-based journalist) is a very gifted writer. Holger Jensen was born in Shanghai, China to a Danish father—who ran a dairy business before the Chinese revolution—and his wife of Slavic Russian ethnicity. His family was kicked out after the Communist takeover; Holger grew up in South Africa. He has been stationed in Moscow, South Vietnam, Hong Kong, South Africa, Beirut, Washington, Toronto, and Miami, and as of 1988, he lived in Denver, working for the *Rocky Mountain News.*"

I went on: "My friend is like many of us, he may be fearful to reveal his gifts, beyond the routines of daily or weekly journalism. When will he learn that he is called and must display his gifts? My guess is that will happen when he makes a commitment to live his life for the Lord... or at least realizes the gifts God has given him, and him alone."

I received some very favorable feedback on the sermon from many, including church secretary Peggy Canody. She had two sons, one of whom was soon to enter seminary. Peggy said I should think about becoming a United Methodist lay speaker. That would allow me to serve in a larger capacity besides singing in our local choir and attending monthly men's breakfasts.

The tradition of lay speaking in the UMC arose from the practice of circuit riding by early Methodists, not only in England led by the Wesley brothers and George Whitefield but also in the original thirteen colonies, where Francis Asbury and Robert Strawbridge, inter alia, rode circuits nearly every weekend to preach at numerous churches in the territory.

One of our contemporary lay-speaking volunteers had a ministry of his own—as a dramatist who memorized many of Strawbridge's sermons and performed frequently for church groups, complete with authentic period clothing. He would brush off imaginary dust from his jacket as he started his sermons, to lend more authenticity.

Peggy gave me the contact details for the two gentlemen in charge of volunteer lay speakers in the Arlington District, Mr. Rob Korte and Mr. Billy Chapman. We became close friends. Rob was a federal civil servant and Billy was a retired senior NCO in the marines. Because of their influence and serious prayer with me and for me, I wrote several paragraphs in my journal on *Why I Want to Be a Lay Speaker*, as follows:

> "To answer the call… to offer my talents for the glory of God and in the service to Christ. To help others learn how they can be saved. To inspire others to live, serve, and achieve according to the needs of His Kingdom. To achieve involvement in many church activities: membership, choir, adult Sunday School, preschool, men's club, liturgist, and lay preaching. I realize I have gifts and obligations to help others. By using and sharing those gifts I help fulfill His purpose for me in this world. By accepting this call and giving myself, I am receiving the promise of eternal life. Faith: The ultimate expression of belief that my life is to be used in service to God as He determines. Faith is active, ever demanding and ever challenging. Faith demands complete surrender to the power of God in working to produce stronger, healthier, and spiritually-gifted human beings. When do I know I have faith? When I can endure setbacks, disappointments, and unexpected events and overcome or master them or manage them without wavering in the steadfast belief in

God's everlasting grace, majesty, and goodness. And faith means never forgetting that 'He is able to humble those who walk in pride.'" (Daniel 4:37b, KJV). Three Ways To Grow: More Bible study; more volunteer speaking; more chances to teach. Three Ways To Help Others: By speaking and challenging others; by helping church organizations; by personal example. The verse Matthew 6:33, KJV applies: 'Seek ye first the Kingdom of God and His righteousness, all these things shall be added unto you.-"

Rob and Billy quickly put me on the rotation for the one continuing ministry opportunity for lay speakers: leading abbreviated Sunday worship services for residents at the Washington House, an upscale assisted-living facility in nearby Alexandria.

Yes, *abbreviated* is the right adjective. Most residents were quite elderly. They gathered for worship on Sundays in a multipurpose room: some completely alert, others in various stages of being distracted or napping and nodding off.

After leading two services, I learned some interesting things. I always wanted to open the service with one or two stanzas from a well-known hymn any attendee might request. I was hoping most of the residents knew the words or enjoyed the hymn. The volunteer pianist, herself a resident, quickly advised me that the best way to encourage singing was to limit the choices to only two or three hymns, saying, "The group doesn't know that hymn" that I may have suggested she play. Whether she was right, or just did not want to learn to play any new hymn, I never knew for sure.

After singing, I usually said a short prayer, gave a brief mini-sermon, and closed with a prayer.

On one occasion, I asked our church's pastor beforehand to bless a small amount of grape juice and some oyster crackers to offer communion to the group. I don't recall how my effort to offer communion went. I do recall the one totally unscripted event during my few times leading such services.

During one opening prayer, as I was speaking, one of the semi-comatose ladies rose up out of her chair and started for the door, exclaiming in a loud voice, "I gotta get out of here!" Maybe my preaching was that bad!

I continued speaking and did my best to rendezvous with her, take her hand, and lead her to the door. Luckily one of the nursing staff was monitoring the service and helped me. I have no idea what the elderly lady's issue was and whether or not it was peacefully resolved.

My mentors Korte and Chapman quickly had me "filling pulpits" in churches around the Arlington District whose pastors were away on occasion. The two mentors also asked me to give my testimony to a large Christian parachurch group who led occasional worship services in various correctional facilities around Fairfax County. I entitled that testimonial sermon "One Man's Wake-Up Call." I received several grateful comments from the group, including a written letter of appreciation from the district superintendent.

I attended a weekend training for the first designation, called Local Church Lay Speakers (LCLS), and was asked the following year to help lead the training for new lay speaking candidates. Because of my participation as an LCLS and as a trainer, I was promoted the next year to CLS—Certified Lay Speaker. I valued both distinctions and of course always mentioned my formal calling was as a lay member and volunteer, certainly without any seminary training.

For the next twelve years, until I left the UMC denomination in 2001, I gave several sermons in many local Methodist churches, including frequent ones at my home church. Some of those sermon titles were *The Road after Bethlehem," "Wholly Faith, Wholly Free," "Fast Food for Five Thousand," "Lessons in a Fishing Boat," "Are Ye Able?" "Christians and Athletes,"* and *"What Did You Get for Christmas?"*

Through friends involved in lay-speaking training, I joined a weekly Bible study (to which I still belong) that was originally part of the Christian Embassy, an outreach ministry in Washington of the Campus Crusade for Christ. The Bible study I attended was geared to professional businessmen and federal employees in the DC area.

Another part of the Christian Embassy had ongoing Bible studies for staffers and Members of Congress on Capitol Hill. Still another part ministered to foreign diplomats stationed at their respective embassies in Washington. The missionaries at the Christian Embassy included women who led similar studies around Washington for female groups. The embassy personnel were stretched very thin from the numerous studies and activities.

A major fundraising activity of the Christian Embassy was an annual golf outing for volunteers at Meadows Farm Golf Course, a very unusual course near Fredericksburg, Virginia. Each volunteer agreed to play one hundred holes of golf (with special arrangements) and sought donors to pledge one dollar a hole, or any other amount per hole.

The initial response when first made aware of the event often was: How could anyone play one hundred holes of golf in a single day, when playing eighteen holes often takes four hours or longer?

But the organizers at the Christian Embassy allowed players to play any of the holes on the course with more than one ball, especially par-3 holes. That is, you could tee off on a par-3 (and as I learned to do when I took to playing solo, on a par-4) hitting two or even three balls off the tee on one hole and playing each ball in succession to the green and in the hole. You were allowed to count the number of balls on each hole. A much quicker way to reach one hundred holes!

Also, the Christian Embassy provided lots and lots of free golf balls. If any shot (numerous, for sure) went out of bounds, landed in water, or became lost, we could throw down another ball as the replacement and count the strokes using that ball. Again, the desire was to speed play and allow players to finish holes at a quicker pace.

The very first year I played, in 2000, I was fortunate to raise the most pledge money of any of the players. First prize was a free set of custom-fitted Titleist irons, a very nice gift. The following years I did not attain the same first place but still raised enough to win other prizes, such as a wet-weather jacket and pants from a major clothing outfitter.

The fundraisers were discontinued shortly after 9/11, much to the disappointment of many. The memories of raising money for a great cause and playing one hundred holes of golf in one day—with caveats—are a great memory.

Another wonderful opportunity to speak and serve as a lay speaker presented itself in 1991. I happened upon a feature article in the *Washington Post* about a Methodist church in one of the poorest sections of Washington, DC, named after the founder of the church, A. P. Shaw, just off Martin Luther King Jr. Avenue SE.

Its second pastor after Reverend Shaw was a charismatic Black preacher my age, Bernard Keels. The article said that he had put up a large sign in the front yard of his church that said simply, SAVING STATION—emphasizing that the ministry of his church was focused on the congregants and neighborhood residents in a large DC neighborhood awash with narcotics trafficking and addiction, out-of-wedlock births and single mothers, and adults of all ages whose inadequate educations deprived most of them of serious job prospects for most of their adult lives.

I invited myself to Pastor Keels's office to share an idea another friend had confided in me: helping many of the young adults in that section of Washington in an intensive, experiential approach centered on a "mountaintop experience" away from their homes. I characterized it as trying to take the slum (i.e., negative thinking) out of the kids, when it is always hard to take the kids out of the slum.

We never developed the idea, but Dr. Keels invited me to participate in his church's Good Friday service that spring. I was one of several lay speakers of his church's lay people in speaking on *The Seven Last Words of Jesus*. A year later, he asked me back to participate again; I was given a different one of the Seven Last Words.

In that first sermon, speaking to an almost entirely African American congregation, I began by holding up my Bible and made the observation aloud that in the Bible, especially the Psalms, "David danced." (Psalm 149:2–3: "Let Israel rejoice in their Maker; let the people of Zion be glad in their King. Let them praise His name with dancing and make music to Him with tambourine and harp.")

I then ended my short introduction, "And in my Bible, this David (me) danced!" Lots of laughter ensued, a good indication that I had managed to warm up my audience.

My exposure to Pastor Keels and the serious spiritual challenges he faced in his community led me to reflect on the words of a famous author of short novels, Og Mandino, and his autobiographical novel *A Better Way to Live*. In one dramatic passage, he wrote,

> "On a dreary winter morning over thirty years ago in Cleveland, a derelict (was) leaning against a cracked pawn shop window. 'The wretch's matted hair hangs down to his shoulders, his eyes bloodshot from the cheap wine he's already consumed that morning. His stomach aches from the lack of food. That man was indeed a failure. Managing within a few short years to lose everything meaningful to him, a loving wife, a beautiful daughter, a nice home, a decent job, plus all his pride, his faith, his confidence, and his self-esteem. Contemplating buying a cheap handgun from the pawn shop and ending his life.'"

Mandino said that such a pitiful human being is commonplace. "That same scenario," Mandino says, "is repeated hundreds of times every day in this beautiful country of ours when people lose their last shred of hope. And that doesn't count the thousands who don't take their lives but give up anyway. They quit on themselves, leading what Thoreau called 'lives of quiet desperation.'"

In other sermons during the mid-1990s, I reflected on some of the same sentiments among others who had lost their way somehow. I wrote in a sermon titled *Wholly Faith, Wholly Free*, such sentiments are as true today as they were twenty-five years ago,

"What is the good news in a country like ours today, where in our families there are a million teenage pregnancies and half a million teenage abortions every year? Where every day, forty teenage mothers give birth to not their first, but their third child? Where every day, one thousand teenagers attempt suicide, and too many succeed? Where is the good news in this country, where in the state of Maryland, there are more college-aged black males in jail than in college?"

I quoted from the story of Jairus in the fifth chapter of the Gospel of Mark: "Jairus was a father whose lovely daughter was either dead, in a deep coma, or in the grip of a strange and probably fatal disease. He sought the Lord, 'I pray thee, Jesus, come and lay thy hands on her, that she may be healed, and she shall live.'"

Jairus is a man who comes to Christ because he is driven by a concern for another life, impelled not so much by his own need as by the desperate need of a loved one. What perhaps he would not have done for himself, he did not hesitate to do for "my little daughter."

The Interpreter's Bible says, "Across the years, the kneeling figure of Jairus says persuasively: 'Keep your mind open. See and venture. Let Jesus bring health and wholeness into life. Let him bring saving power into a civilization gone into a deathlike coma.'"

I continued, and find it a universal truth in today's America in the twenty-first century as well:

"There are parents all over America today who have something they're pretending not to know, perhaps their own failures in the lives of others. Like the alcoholic father and thousands of other parents who have learned the awful truths behind their teenagers' drug habits or despair or suicides—these people will never be wholly free until they demonstrate their willingness to submit to God, wholly on faith. Many will take their burdens to the grave, and many are, for all intents and purposes, dead spiritually right now, unaware of the relief of confession and the joy of wholly faith, wholly free."

That was my Father's Day sermon, delivered in my home church. In another Father's Day sermon there two years later, I took on the issue of abortion, citing comments made by Mother Teresa and Pope John Paul II. Each of them lectured then–President Clinton on two separate occasions ten months apart. Pope John Paul II on one occasion said, "The inalienable dignity of every human being and the rights which flow from that dignity, including the right to life and the defense of life, are at the heart of the church's message and action in the world."

I received some negative feedback from some in the congregation, but I was buoyed by the comment from one church member, a retired chief of chaplains in the US Navy, the late Captain Robert Radcliffe, who exclaimed, "Wow, I didn't think anyone else would dare preach a powerful sermon like that in this church!"

A few months earlier at a National Prayer Breakfast in Washington, Mother Teresa said that abortion was the greatest destroyer of peace today. "Many people are very, very concerned with the children of India, with the children of Africa where quite a few die of hunger, and so on… But often these same people are not concerned with the millions who are being killed by the deliberate decision of their own mothers and fathers."

Besides the enjoyment and spiritual growth I experienced from the numerous lay-preaching opportunities, I also was fortunate to lead an adult Sunday school class for a few years. I led the discussions among eight to ten regular attendees on Sunday mornings. I especially loved the short novels of Og Mandino, among them *The Greatest Salesman in the World*; *The Greatest Miracle in the World* (perhaps my favorite for its "God Memorandum" at the end of the book); *The Return of the Ragpicker*; and *The Christ Commission*, a historical novel that dwells even more extensively on biblical times than the others.

Another book I led discussions on was *Parables from the Back Side* by J. Ellsworth Kalas. The title revealed the self-evident contents. And of course, I thoroughly enjoyed the few weeks we spent discussing the classic novel *In His Steps* by Charles Sheldon that became the genesis for the ubiquitous expression "What would Jesus do?" WWJD.

I left the UMC denomination in 2001, and in quick succession (largely because of pastoral changes), I joined the Calvary Church of the Nazarene (a wonderful denomination) and then McLean Bible Church, the megachurch referred to elsewhere.

Mother and daughter with Michael W. Smith,
Christmas concert, McLean Bible Church, 2012.

I was no longer a certified lay speaker and forfeited most opportunities to speak and to lead adult Sunday school classes. But I treasure the very significant growth I experienced in the preparation and delivery of many sermons and the help I may have been able to provide in other peoples' lives. As one believer put it, "Christianity is nothing more than one beggar telling another beggar where to find food." To which I would add the one-liner from one of the Christian radio stations, "If you don't like adventure, the life of faith is not for you."

\#   \#   \#

CHAPTER 25

Trips to The Former Soviet Union, 1992–1994

THE LAST CHAPTER dealt with much of my spiritual journey well into the decade of the 1990s. I was engaged during that decade in professional pursuits that included a limited time producing documentary video programming during a three-year assignment (1992–1994) at the Department of State. I was not a career foreign service officer—rather, a government contractor working on our country's assistance programs to the former Soviet Union (New Independent States). After that term in government, I ended the decade in the private sector as a country director in Thailand for my West Point classmate John Wing and his company, The Wing Group, developing independent power plants in Southeast Asia.

The work as a documentary television producer carried over from a brief contract with a small government contractor supporting the US Army Reserve Command at Fort Belvoir; the experience morphed into a series of feature-length (up to a half hour) documentaries on the American government's assistance program in the NIS. Two of my documentaries won honorable mention awards, one from the WorldFest-Houston International

Film Festival and the other from the Charleston, South Carolina, International Film Festival.

Those two productions showed the unusual nature of our assistance program that reminded the elder generations of the Marshall Plan, which helped rebuild Western Europe after World War II.

The Department of State work began in the first months of 1992. The USSR had collapsed; in January, a major international pledging conference was attended by many nations. A new office at the Department of State was established, reporting directly to Deputy Secretary Lawrence Eagleburger and managed by my former boss at the Pentagon, newly-appointed Ambassador Richard Armitage.

The first task under the new office was to manage and coordinate the emergency humanitarian assistance airlift, code-named Operation Provide Hope, to deliver tons of emergency food and medicines to all twelve NIS.

> The US Air Force Air Mobility Command Museum website says that "On January 23, 1992, Secretary of State James Baker announced Provide Hope, an operation to deliver massive amounts of aid to the CIS. Congress appropriated $100 million for relief for the former Soviet republics, and Baker knew that large quantities of food and medicine were available from stockpiles left after the Persian Gulf conflict in 1991 … Provide Hope I transported 2,274 tons of food and medical supplies to 24 cities in 10 former Soviet republics. All but 417 tons of the cargo was food, which came from warehouses in Pisa, Italy, and Rotterdam in the Netherlands. The food included beef, ham, pork, chicken, fish, potatoes, rice, vegetables, pasta, bread, and beverages. The remaining supplies were medical, and included bandages, sutures, adhesive tape, cotton, surgical sponges, disposable gloves, patients' clothing, blankets, and sheets. The medical cargo

came from the Army Medical Materiel Center at Pirmasens, Germany, and from the United Kingdom. Convoys of trucks transported the food and medical supplies to three aerial ports of embarkation: Rhein-Main AB in Germany and Incirlik AB and Ankara Air Station (AS) in Turkey. Military Airlift Command aircraft flew 46 C-141 and 19 C-5 flights… during the 17 days of Provide Hope I. Of these missions, 22 went to Russia; 7 each to Armenia and Kazakhstan; 5 to Ukraine; 4 each to Turkmenistan, Azerbaijan, Tajikistan, and Uzbekistan; 3 flights each to Kyrgyzstan and Moldova; and 2 *to* Belarus.

The operation began with seventeen separate flights to disparate NIS destinations on February 10. I escorted several reporters wanting to cover the first deliveries. We flew into Moscow aboard a US Air Force C-5 Galaxy from Rhein-Main Air Base in Germany. We arrived early that morning at snow-covered Domodedovo Airport. The air force crew offloaded the food and medicines without any serious delay, and within a few hours the C-5 aircraft was en route back to Rhein-Main AB. One or two reporters who had wanted to stay in Moscow were allowed to stay but had to possess Russian visas and be able to handle their own departures from Moscow.

Rather than schedule myself on any successive flights, I boarded the superefficient Deutsche Bahn train from Frankfurt to Stuttgart and the headquarters of the US European Command (EUCOM) to coordinate ongoing interagency efforts and media arrangements with EUCOM offices. My temporary senior-level rank allowed me to stay overnight in the EUCOM VIP officers' suite named for retired US Army General Andrew Goodpaster (USMA 1939). He had led the European Command in the early 1970s. EUCOM staff issued me several items of Arctic clothing including a parka, thermal underwear, gloves, and headgear, presupposing my winter travels into some of the NIS.

Working in a wintry weather environment was quite different from all my previous overseas work, first in Vietnam, then stationed in Thailand, and afterward traveling on numerous assignments in tropical to moderate temperatures mostly throughout South and Southeast Asia.

The next three years comprised a heady experience filled with numerous memorable vignettes and "drinking from a fire hose" learning so much history, sociology, arts and culture, and economics in the home of what had been America's major Cold War enemy.

In the coming spring of 1992, our office's active role in Operation Provide Hope dwindled; the Pentagon assumed aerial and overland shipments into the twelve NIS. The US Congress appropriated new funds beyond the emergency authorization of $100 million for Operation Provide Hope. The authorization said new funds would be used for a variety of technical assistance, to be implemented by numerous US government agencies and other contractors.

The new legislation totaled more than $400 million in economic support funds under the FREEDOM Support Act—FREEDOM was the wordy acronym Freedom for Russia and Emerging Eurasian Democracies and Open Markets! The authorization was modeled after its slightly older sister, the SEED Act of 1989—SEED standing for Support for East European Democracies (the Communist satellite regimes prior to the fall of the Iron Curtain).

Our office's role became larger in managing the variety of implementing agencies and contractors. We added several new employees, most of them career State Department foreign service officers, to act as "account executives" for the various types of technical assistance and the assigned agencies and contractors.

One of the benefits I realized under the new legislation was the opportunity to create an aggressive public diplomacy effort in the United States through various world council and civic organizations in many major cities. Our office was allowed to use a small portion of the appropriated funds to reach out to civic organizations in American cities to publicize private-sector opportunities in the entire assistance program.

I worked with the permanent public diplomacy office at the State Department—chiefly by having one of our office "account executives" speak at one of their regular events. I organized three regional visits from the West Coast to the Rocky Mountain states and the Midwest and worked with three colleagues from the US Agency for International Development (USAID): Jim Schill, an old friend from my hometown of Sioux City, Iowa; and two of his supervisors in the Bureau of Private Enterprise, Director Ralph Blackman and Deputy Director John Wilkinson. Jim's major assignment during the Vietnam War more than twenty years earlier was as a USAID program officer in Laos (who constantly regaled me with his many war stories about the frontier days in Laos). He and I made our first acquaintance in 1979 in Singapore, where he was a refugee assistance officer helping Vietnamese boat people showing up in the island nation. That event is described elsewhere. Jim and I had graduated from the same high school in Sioux City. Through his friendship, I became close professional and personal friends with the other two senior USAID officers, Ralph and John.

Our first public diplomacy foray was a West Coast speaking tour. USAID had assigned Jim as the USAID outreach officer to set up and manage West Coast public-private sector partnerships. Ralph Blackman and I spent five days in July with Jim; we spoke to civic audiences in Portland, Oregon; Seattle, Washington; and the California cities of San Jose, Ontario/Inland Empire, and San Diego. We had excellent turnouts in each city. We scheduled two more tours in the next few months—a Rocky Mountain tour in Colorado, Utah, and Idaho, and a Midwest tour in Iowa, Illinois, and Wisconsin. Those two regional tours were similarly well attended. (My biggest personal thrill was having my parents attend the program in Des Moines—where they had first met fifty years earlier, before World War II, and where our family lived before moving to Sioux City in 1952. Old home week for Mom and Dad and me! I recognized my parents in my opening remarks with the advertising slogan for Old Milwaukee beer: "It doesn't get any better than this!" True statement.)

The most exciting off-schedule event of all three tours occurred after our last Rocky Mountain stop in Pocatello, Idaho. A close friend had arranged for me to spend the long weekend in Yellowstone National Park. He was a former tour guide all over Idaho and Wyoming, so he knew Yellowstone very well. With one or two other close friends of his, we parked our cars along the highway adjacent to Lewis Lake and took our canoes across the lake and part of the way along a narrow stream leading to Shoshone Lake. Because of the shallowness of the stream, we had to stash the canoes in the brush midway along and portage all our supplies the rest of the way. My friend and guide Targhee James (named after the Targhee National Forest in Idaho) had organized all supplies, not just sleeping bags, fly-fishing equipment, and food but also a fully capable cooking tent with a small portable stove and a tepee for a fire with hot stones one evening in a Native American sauna. One night after midnight, we disrobed and sank our bodies into a couple of small, warm geysers. Wild animals in the nearby forests serenaded our late-night soiree. Two of the days we spent fly-fishing in the lake and the stream for speckled trout, rainbow trout, and cutthroat trout. A great weekend.

As winter approached, officers from the military unit in the Pentagon responsible for joint inspections of many heretofore top-secret nuclear facilities in Russia solicited our office to advance the entire assistance program. That office, the On-Site Inspection Agency (OSIA), wanted to send a camera crew and interpreter with me during the Orthodox holiday season of 1992–1993 to acquire video footage and still photos of the distribution of humanitarian supplies, chiefly food rations and medicines. The intended recipients were either numerous families living below the poverty level or approved charity offices in Moscow and St. Petersburg.

The ten days or so in Russia during Orthodox Christmas was a fascinating look into any society's intrinsic human struggle to survive in the two most well-known Russian cities.

The two most memorable families I met in Moscow were on both sides of the delivery machinery, giving and receiving, through a consortium of relief agencies, to include the Moscow office of CARE, the Salvation Army, and many other Christian and Jewish relief agencies, plus others.

The American embassy suggested we introduce ourselves to the first such family, the manager of the Salvation Army office, Mr. Sven Ljungholm, and his wife, Kathy. The couple had relinquished a corporate lifestyle and Sven's position as the Scandinavian Air Lines station manager in New York City to follow in the footsteps of Sven's grandfather, who had established the first Salvation Army office in Moscow just after the Russian Revolution (1917–1923). Sven agreed to allow our camera crew to follow volunteers on one or two occasions, and we readily agreed.

On the Sunday morning we were there, I was fortunate enough to attend Salvation Army worship services in a school gymnasium in Moscow. I recall little else of the service, e.g., whether or not portions of the service were in English and portions in Russian.

We spent Orthodox Christmas Eve at the largest Orthodox church. A light snowfall welcomed hundreds of observants arriving for the Vespers service, inside a picturesque church with no seats in the auditorium. Observants stood for the entire worship service, listening to the clergy and chanting.

Foreign diplomats and other expats said that many common citizens in Russia continued to view the Orthodox Church with suspicion, believing that the leadership of the Orthodox Church collaborated with the Communist regime since the revolution.

By far the most dramatic Salvation Army delivery of emergency humanitarian supplies took place on another evening a short walk from the Radisson Hotel that had begun business the previous year. Within a few blocks of the front door was one of nine rail stations in Moscow, the Kiev (Kievsky) Rail Station. Prior to that night, we had noticed long queues of elderly adults, mostly women, in whatever cold-weather gear they could manage, standing in lines in the plaza adjacent to the station and selling a variety of used household items.

The rapid dissolution of the USSR had meant almost instant and often severe poverty for many pensioners, such as this group. The Russian ruble was virtually worthless, and domestic factories and food-processing facilities were unable to ensure any reasonable flow of food to the population.

Medicines were also largely nonexistent. The Soviet Union had depended upon their Eastern European satellite countries for pharmaceuticals and most medical supplies. With the collapse of the currency, imports of all these medicines and medical supplies had dried up. Other observations of medical care in the former Soviet Union follow later in this memoir, describing visits to various hospitals during the summer of the same year.

The desperate line outside the train station was selling used clothing, grooming items, and tools. And perhaps the most heartbreaking sight, one lady was trying to sell a half-empty tube of toothpaste for whatever few rubles or foreign currency she could attract. Scenes like this were commonplace at the time, and each scene led to large and small heartbreaks among visitors like us.

The night in question, we met a dozen uniformed Salvation Army volunteers who were carrying portable containers of hot beverages and simple pastries for their tour inside the train station to hand out to travelers and others. We followed the volunteers as they descended from the main level to lower levels and terminals for rail routes, including not only to the Ukrainian capital but also to Vnukovo International Airport.

We descended to the lowest level possible, where we came upon truly miserable circumstances: homeless families, numbering hundreds of people of all ages. None of them were travelers or waiting for trains. Instead, their permanent residence was in front of us, spread out everywhere. Sven said that most of these families had been living underground at the train station for years, and apparently many, if not most, had never been aboveground or seen the outdoors. They lived and died far underground in a train station.

The volunteers moved among the settlers as best they could, trying to serve hot beverages and pastries to as many as they could serve, or telling penurious families that other volunteers were coming by very shortly.

I can never erase from my memory the homeless hundreds living hand-to-mouth in the dungeon-like basement level of the Kiev Rail Station. I have no idea if conditions have improved to any degree that allow new generations to extract themselves from such wretched conditions.

On another day, our crew accompanied Sven's wife, Kathy, during her frequent visits to several Moscow orphanages. I didn't know the exact number of orphanages in the Moscow area, but they must have been numerous. We did not do an exhaustive interview with any of the managers or other personnel at any one orphanage to learn anecdotal experiences or ask about the apparently large number of orphans in Moscow, and probably in other cities.

As I would learn later that year, the most common birth-control method for Russian women was abortion. It was not unusual to hear of women having up to a half dozen or more abortions each and suffering tremendous mental anguish from so many terminated pregnancies.

The most striking element of our visit to orphanages was that each had many tiny orphans, abandoned by parents unable to afford new mouths, lying without crying in small cribs or beds, usually in one large but completely quiet ward. Kathy Ljungholm said that the babies' cries for food or milk usually went unheeded. The attendants had almost nothing to offer to relieve the hunger and ignored the cries. So, the babies learned to conserve what little energy they had by remaining quiet all the time. Presumably they received infant formula mealtimes, provided by foreign donors.

The most dramatic and heartwarming distribution of humanitarian assistance concerned the second family in my memoir. It happened on a very dark evening in a nondescript and ubiquitous apartment building in a far suburb of Moscow. The local office of CARE provided a list of deserving (i.e., living under the stated poverty line) families needing assistance. We climbed the crumbling indoor steps to visit a family. As we neared the door on the third or fourth floor, recorded music with American voices wafted down. To the surprise of all of us, the music was American gospel music!

Our party included six of us Americans in the camera party and three or four Russian ladies either from CARE or from one of the few "vetted"

Russian NGOs distributing family food packages. (American embassy officers had said that the concept of NGO in the former Soviet Union was a misnomer: any supposed NGO was little more than one person, or a small number of people, labeling itself as an NGO, but without any altruism. Rather, such petty thieves had been able to convince a donor entity, domestic or foreign, to donate supplies or money supposedly intended for some needy group. Instead, the supplies and any cash were usually stolen for the enrichment of that group.)

The family we overwhelmed that night was certainly deserving, however, as we learned within a few minutes of our crowding into the apartment: a three-bedroom apartment (the third bedroom was a ridiculously small "maid's quarters" behind the kitchen, where the husband and wife slept). The family included the wife's mother and eight children, if memory serves.

One of the two regular bedrooms housed the wife's mother and the couple of female children. The other bedroom housed two of the older male children. And right there in the living room, in a double bunk bed, slept the four youngest sons. To say *crowded* was an understatement, and again, with our temporary invasion, the scene was a mini-madhouse.

That day had also been the husband's birthday. The wife had spent the day, as most Soviet-era wives did back then, waiting in lines at every sort of food outlet that may or may not have foodstuffs and groceries. Fortunately, she succeeded in buying a small birthday cake for the occasion; we were invaders at the family birthday party.

I never did ask my American military interpreter, Sam Cowan, to ask the names of either spouse, much less any of the children. (Nor did I ever learn how the family had obtained the American gospel recordings.) I named the husband Sergei to use when referring to him. Adding more drama to the entire incident, Sergei was blind. I do not remember if he happened to tell us, or if the ladies viewing the food package handover had told us, how long he had been without sight.

We celebrated the birthday with small slices of birthday cake and some tiny amounts of fruit punch or lemonade. The portions were divided up to serve more than twice the mouths the mother had been expecting. The music continued to play in the background.

Many of the children, with Sam translating, were taking impromptu turns calling out elements of famous Bible stories: out of the mouths of babes in an almost-surreal home Sunday school setting. And an amazing spiritual moment to God's omnipresence in a very humble and, for that evening, super-crowded abode.

Before we left, I asked Sam, himself a believer, to translate for Sergei's benefit as another fellow believer, "Someday we will be in heaven together."

Sam took great literary license with my request and instead said, "Dave wants to tell you that someday, you and he will walk the golden streets of heaven together!" Sergei replied, "I believe that!"

An unbelievable end to a spectacular spiritual encounter in an over-crowded Russian apartment—thanks be to God.

And someday the two of us—this sinner named Dave Hatcher and a blind Russian believer I will always call Sergei, who shared his extremely limited resources with us and having been born into Soviet Communism about the same time I was being born in a modern American hospital—will indeed walk the golden streets of heaven together! "What a day of rejoicing that'll be" in the words of the famous hymn *When We All Get to Heaven.* "When we all see Jesus, we'll sing and *shout* the victory!"

#   #   #

The train trip to St. Petersburg was uneventful except for two anecdotes. We spent a cold Saturday morning touring the world-famous Hermitage Museum, a wonderful treat for all of us. We easily could have spent many hours on several floors admiring the fantastic collections of Russian and European art.

The second anecdote was our luxurious two-night stay in the five-star Europa Hotel, Our entire crew appreciated the heated bathroom tiles, a great benefit in a city closer than Moscow to the North Pole. Fortunately, our per diem hotel allowances covered the room rental rates at the Europa and many other hotels coming on line in the NIS.

A few years later while on a personal business trip in Asia, I was watching the movie *GoldenEye* starring Pierce Brosnan. I recognized several street scenes from my brief stay in St. Petersburg.

One last comment: Vladimir Putin was a senior KGB officer in St. Petersburg before his publicized retirement in 1991. I have no idea whether or not he was there in 1993. Obviously, I would not have been able to identify him if our camera crew had somehow stumbled upon him during our trip.

However, I recall that thirteen years earlier, on a CBS News assignment in the Laotian capital of Vientiane to cover the fifth year under Communism, we stumbled upon another Soviet representative completely unknown abroad at the time: Mikhail Gorbachev.

There was a cynical anti-Communist joke making the rounds that the tallest building in Moscow was the four-story Lubyanka Building, headquarters of the KGB, where political prisoners were imprisoned in underground floors. The joke said that the KGB building was the tallest in Moscow: from the basement, one could see all the way to Siberia!

Within a few months, a different American military camera crew and a new interpreter would accompany me on a visit to document the human face of many American volunteers involved in several technical assistance projects. We spent time not only in Moscow but in two more Russian cities on either side of the Ural Mountains and in the environs of the capitals of Ukraine and Armenia.

Before that trip, however, I was fortunate enough to invite Sven and Kathy Ljungholm to my home church in Virginia as guest speakers on their experiences in Russia. They graciously accepted my invitation.

After that visit by the Ljungholms, I flew back to the NIS to document more assistance programs in Moscow and other locations. I received professional photo and video support from the US Air Force headquarters in Europe, plus a new interpreter from the On-Site Inspection Agency.

Like his colleague Sam Cowan on the earlier trip, Yuri Boguslavsky was an unforgettable character. At the time, he was twenty-eight years old. He grew up in Moscow until the age of fourteen. His parents were musicians. The family migrated to the US during his teenage years, living first in New York City and later in Salt Lake City.

Yuri was completely bilingual and a perfect interpreter/translator. During our three weeks together, his assistance and his quirky sense of humor were valuable additions. He loved scouring bookstores and open-air impromptu markets when possible, searching for Russian-language joke books.

One of his jokes featured the Reagan-Gorbachev summit in 1986 in Iceland. During a break in the discussions, the joke went, three of the four main luminaries were relaxing in a hotel suite.

> The joke: President Reagan playfully asked his secretary of state, George Schultz, "George, who's your mother's son but not your brother?" Schultz thought for a while and said, "Why, that's me!" Reagan nodded in the affirmative. Soviet Chairman Gorbachev hurried out of the suite and ran into Boris Yeltsin in the hall, excitedly saying, "Boris, Boris, who's your mother's son but not your brother?" Yeltsin thinks for a few seconds and says, "Why, that's me."
>
> To which Gorbachev replied, "No, you idiot! It's Schultz!"

When our small crew arrived in Moscow, American diplomats helped us plan an itinerary in the cities of Nizhny Novgorod and Yekaterinburg. Other American diplomats in Armenia and Ukraine would do the same for us. We boarded the overnight train to the first city, Nizhny Novgorod, nick-named Nizhny. During the Communist rule from 1932 to 1990, the same city had the name of Gorky and served as an internal exile city for political prisoners. I was briefed in Washington by officers of the International Finance Corporation (IFC) office, a division of the World Bank, about IFC technical assistance projects in Nizhny. Their branch office was in the large Soviet-era hotel on a hill overlooking the confluence of the Volga River with its small tributary, the Oka.

Our first surprise came when we approached the hotel front desk to request rooms. The receptionist said that there were no rooms available, even though IFC staff said there were numerous vacancies in the large Soviet-era hotel. We turned away to consider options. An expatriate of uncertain nationality approached us and warned us to be careful while in Nizhny.

He claimed that a close friend had ventured from the hotel on a recent evening. Local thugs supposedly victimized that friend and stole almost all of his clothing and valuables before he could get back to the hotel. No one knows the truth, but his story was a harbinger of things to come.

Our protests to stay at the almost-empty hotel fell on deaf ears. The receptionist explained that without advance reservations, we were not entitled to lodging! It became clear that the further removed one was from Moscow, business principles such as renting out unsold hotel rooms, etc., even at the last minute, were foreign concepts to Russians managing commercial properties.

IFC personnel in the hotel recommended we move to the Central Hotel, a smaller hotel downtown that housed Peace Corps volunteers. Luckily, there was no such problem at the Central Hotel. We would soon learn why.

We hurried down to the Central Hotel to check in. The facade and entrance of the hotel revealed it to be a well-worn two-star or three-star hotel. In the lobby, the scene was reminiscent of *Star Wars*: a collection of middle-aged or younger "toughs" lounging on the available sofas and chairs, with no women or families in sight. The Peace Corps manager had warned us over the phone that the hotel was a favorite "office" for many Georgian "entrepreneurs" with moneymaking schemes, without being more specific.

After check-in, we struggled with putting our luggage and equipment into the small, spartan elevator. The next surprise: in such "colorful" hotels, managers often hired floor matrons to police the floors. In our case, our matron was at her desk near the elevator as we began manhandling our luggage and equipment while figuring out where our rooms were. The matron controlled one or two porters who seemed to lack a high school education.

As we started to push and shove our gear down the hall, Yuri heard the matron shout in Russian to the porters: "Hey, I told you to help these people! They're Americans, not Armenians!" Obviously, ethnic Armenians were looked upon with some disfavor in provincial Russia, for whatever reason.

At the end of our short stay in Nizhny, we were required to submit to a room inspection by the same matron. Commonplace burglaries and petty thievery of room accoutrements required room inspections for all guests. Even the black-and-white television sets, with static in most flickering images, were chained and bolted down!

Neither the IFC staff nor the Peace Corps had any tangible projects at the time, or anything else of visual appeal. We did a couple of interviews to have videotape for postproduction purposes.

One memorable highlight in Nizhny was a boat trip on the Volga one afternoon. I wanted to have video and still images of the famous river and scenes of life along the river, to show ordinary life while citizens everywhere in the NIS struggled with their independence.

We were able to hire a female guide for our boat ride. She arranged a riverboat and captain for something like eight dollars for the hour: an indication of very little river traffic and disappointing economic conditions.

Our guide was actually from Estonia. She was happy to earn whatever we were paying her. The hour on the Volga was refreshing and relaxing. All of us foreigners were enjoying ourselves. Our laid-back behavior and easy laughter led the Estonian lady to express disbelief that Americans, and presumably other Westerners, could be so happy all the time.

It seemed to me that in the former Soviet Union, adults had forgotten how to smile. Their lives in general rarely allowed for any true enjoyment and laughter. I had the impression that the facial muscles of many if not most adults were frozen in place from chronic frowning or unending sadness and depression.

We left Nizhny on the overnight train back to Moscow, but the memories of both Nizhny hotels, and the comment by the Estonian lady, remain with me to this day.

We decided that our next destination should be Yekaterinburg, a two-hour flight east that crossed over the Ural Mountains that separated the two parts of the country. We wanted to visit any project that was receiving foreign assistance. We ended up traveling an hour to visit a factory in the town of Asbest that was forging concrete blocks and bricks for commercial construction.

The Aeroflot flight was a Russian version of a wide-bodied Airbus. Our lodging in the city was a largely vacant school dormitory (in July). The rooms were small, and there were very few bathroom facilities along the hallways.

My main memory occurred on the return from Asbest. We stopped along the road to view the ruins of a former Russian Orthodox church. The church had been ravaged several years earlier. Almost all the flooring and all furniture and even the exterior doors had been removed or ripped out. Much of the structure showed significant fire damage. Large sections of roofing were missing.

But as we walked tightrope style along the heavy floor joists, I happened to look up at the beams supporting what ceiling remained. Along the beams, and still evident in some of the wooden ceiling panels, were painted Christian symbols and Orthodox icons of their Savior and mine, the Christ child.

To me, it was a testament, on the side of a remote country road east of the Ural Mountains: even the spirit-killing nature of atheistic Communism could not completely erase the universal meaning of life promised by the Triune God of Father, Son, and Holy Spirit. I remember humming the melody and voicing some of the words to the great hymn "Simply and Tenderly, Jesus Is Calling." I thanked God for the many exposures during my fairly new spiritual journey and for His omnipresence in the form of striking encounters like this one on the backroads of Siberia.

Back in Moscow for a day or two, we prepared for the stops in Armenia and Ukraine.

Our landing in Yerevan on the Aeroflot flight was eventful. The seating in one large cabin aboard our propeller-driven aircraft was numerous rows from front to back in only one cabin. It seemed that ethnic Armenians occupied almost all of the seats. They were returning to Yerevan from buying trips to Moscow to resell all manner of consumer goods.

We stood up to begin to disembark. A flight attendant came on the intercom and excitedly ordered the Armenians to remain in their seats to allow the Russian pilots to leave first. The cockpit crew came running down the center aisle to the rear exit! We foreigners and ethnic Russians such as Yuri were allowed to deplane before the Armenians, with their numerous carry on bags and who knows what in the baggage compartment!

One of the projects near Yerevan that we documented was an agricultural project under the auspices of the American NGO VOCA, Volunteers in Overseas Cooperative Assistance. Volunteers were advising farmers on ways to increase yields, eliminate pests, and kill off plant diseases.

Our local escorts took the time to point out a mountain range in the distance, near the border with Turkey and centered on Mount Ararat, the supposed landing place of Noah's Ark. A traveler in 2015 wrote on a popular travel website, "[Mount Ararat] is easily visible from the Armenian side of the border. Sometimes on hazy days it is hard to see the mountain from Yerevan, but on a sunny day it hovers so hugely over the city that it is hard to imagine it being obscured at all. Ararat is a beautiful geological wonder!"

The other special highlight was our visit to the headquarters of the Armenian Apostolic (Orthodox) Church in Etchmiadzin, also known as Vagharshapat. St. Gregory the Illuminator built the Etchmiadzin Cathedral between 301 CE and 303 CE. It is considered one of the oldest churches in the world. We had the good fortune to visit and tour the interior.

Deep in the basement among other relics was what church historians claim is the Holy Lance—the spear that Roman soldiers used to pierce the body of Christ just before His crucifixion. Two other spears said by others outside Armenia to be the Holy Lance are in St. Peter's Basilica in the Vatican and in Vienna, Austria. The Armenian Holy Lance is kept behind plexiglass, making it virtually impossible for outsiders to judge the authenticity.

A final Yerevan memory was a poignant interview with a young African-American female Peace Corps volunteer. She spoke of the enormous privations their group experienced the previous winter, in their small and sparsely furnished rooms, without sufficient heating. She spoke of many days and evenings when the cold penetrated everything. The only warm location in the entire capital was the Yerevan Opera Theatre that had re-opened. That was the explanation for the extremely high theater attendance almost every night!

Once back in Moscow, our crew had one more visit to schedule to complete our extensive three-week assignment documenting many human faces of altruism.

The short flight to Ukraine's capital, Kiev or Kyiv, was noneventful. We checked into the Hotel Rus, one of the few functioning hotels at the time. The Encyclopedia says that the Kievan Rus for whom the hotel was named was the first East Slavic state that reached its peak in the early 11th Century. The hotel was basic and nondescript. It overlooked the Olympiyskiy National Sports Complex and stadium.

We wanted to visit two projects, one in the capital and one near the city of Bellekirche, translated "beautiful church", a few hours away by car.

American workers from Pueblo, Colorado, were fulfilling a contract to teach farmers how to construct Quonset huts, quintessential American storage buildings for crops and other possessions.

A team of engineers at Quonset Point Naval Air Station in Rhode Island had designed the huts in 1941. The huts were easily constructed using corrugated sheet metal. The workers gladly welcomed our English-speaking crew and fell all over themselves offering us imported packaged snacks and beer.

On the road back to the capital, we stopped briefly, where I unknowingly consumed my first meal of fresh roadkill! An elderly villager had set up his makeshift smoker using rough pieces of charcoal to roast whatever flesh he could recover from animals trapped in nearby vegetation. We lived dangerously: if the heat was high enough for thoroughly cooking the meat, we thought we risked little chance of food poisoning as we dined on genuine Ukrainian country barbecue! We were lucky.

The project in the capital was the initial establishment of Internews, an independent news media operation with branches not only in Ukraine but in other NIS under the international NGO Internews. Whatever its success has been, its website in 2023 promotes "a wide range of issues, including: confronting propaganda and corruption; protecting a free and open internet; educating citizens on media and data literacy; and strengthening health and environmental systems."

We did brief interviews with local staff and gathered footage of the office and local street scenes. We finally called it quits from Ukraine and the other recent locations: Moscow, Nizhny-Novgorod, and Yekaterinburg in Russia; Yerevan and Etchmiazin in Armenia; and Kiev or Kyiv and Bellekirche.

One final Moscow note. The two Western food outlets already well established in 1993 were two separate McDonald's locations and a Pizza Hut within a few minutes walk from the Radisson Hotel. The unique feature of the Pizza Hut was its division. Two sides served customers, a hard-currency section and one for customers with Russian rubles.

Seating in the hard-currency section was almost always available, and the service was quite satisfactory. The lines to get into the Russian rubles section were always much, much longer. Since we always frequented the section accepting American dollars, we have no way of knowing about the service or quality of pizza in the other section.

Our crew split up quickly after the three week endeavor. The camera crew returned to their unit in Germany. Yuri Boguslavsky and I flew back to Dulles Airport; his unit, the On-Site Inspection Agency, was on the airport property.

On the Delta Airlines flight from Frankfurt, I began reading the late P. J. O'Rourke's hilarious satire *Holidays in Hell*—just a few days after three weeks visiting some destinations resembling the title. Or as Fred Hof, another close colleague in the same State Department office at the time, said, talking about the capital of Azerbaijan: "You're not at the end of the earth in Baku—but you can certainly see it from there!"

Anyway, I remember laughing so hard reading *Holidays in Hell* inside the crowded Delta Airlines cabin so often that I drew looks of curiosity, disgust, or vicarious enjoyment from many passengers. Disruptive, yes. Unintentional, ditto. But I could not help comparing his audacious and witty prose with my own observations of life in the NIS in 1993.

I set to work back in the office on scriptwriting and postproduction work on the documentary and on the distribution of the still photos and captions. The final thirty-minute documentary received an honorable mention at the annual Houston WorldFest Film Festival.

The other momentous experience before leaving the State Department in 1994 was my producing another video effort involving time in New Mexico, Moscow, and St. Petersburg. *Topaz* was the code name of a joint deep-space exploration project that was authorized under the Nunn-Lugar legislation that governed nuclear cooperation. *Topaz* became a joint research effort between both countries' top nuclear scientists to study the feasibility of developing nuclear power for deep-space exploration.

The biggest American champion for the project, for good reason, was the senior US senator from New Mexico, the late Pete Domenici. The focus for the American effort was centered on the two centers of brainpower in New Mexico: Sandia National Laboratory in Albuquerque and Los Alamos National Laboratory in Los Alamos.

I flew to Albuquerque to meet scientists at the Sandia National Laboratory (hereafter Sandia Lab) under the leadership of chief scientist Frank Thome. His team was studying the demands of the actual project and what hospitality was allowable for the Russian scientists and families (and undoubtedly one or more ex-KGB officers). Frank and his team enjoyed my personal recounting of my recent visits to Russia and the other new independent states.

On a follow-up visit to Albuquerque, I requested to bring Yuri Boguslavsky with me. He served up his special brand of Russian humor to the great enjoyment of the Americans at Sandia Lab.

New Mexico is a very fascinating state with its mix of cultures going back to Mexican and Native American influences, and white Americans in a fairly large Jewish migration in the late nineteenth century. According to the website for the New Mexico Jewish Historical Society:

> New Mexico's Jewish history reaches back almost five hundred years when some of the early Spanish arrivals by way of Mexico traced their family histories to Spanish and Portuguese Sephardic Jews who became *conversos*, or "converted" in order to escape the clutches of the Spanish Inquisition. Today, a number of Hispanic descendants are exploring their families' crypto-Jewish roots.
>
> The mid-nineteenth century marked the arrival of European Ashkenazi Jews via the Santa Fe Trail, and they became the leading merchants in the territory. When the railroad arrived in the 1880s, more Jewish merchants arrived and expanded their business presence throughout New Mexico. The history of New Mexico Jews tells the stories of individuals and organizations who made their mark on all walks of life from business/commerce; ranchers and miners; social organizations; traders with the Navajo and Pueblo reservations; to becoming the first mayor of Albuquerque and first governor of the state. All of them made significant contributions to the territory and later state, and it is our goal and responsibility to ensure the recognition as well as through educational programming this rich history reaches the public. New Mexico Jewish history, therefore, reflects a

blend of both Ashkenazi and Sephardic cultural traditions, a unique feature in US Jewish history."

There were large numbers of settlers from Mexico along with a variety of Native American tribes' families of Apache, Navajo, and Santa Clara Pueblo tribes who constructed and lived in the impressive Puye Cliff Dwellings outside Los Alamos. Other ancestral Puebloans settled in and around what is now Bandelier National Monument.

I mention Puye and Bandelier for a reason. Just before that first trip to Albuquerque, I reconnected with a former high school friend living there. She and her husband spent a Sunday showing me around the Puye Cliff Dwellings for a short course on the cliff dwelling and the state's history. During my second visit to the state, Yuri Boguslavsky and I spent one Saturday touring Bandelier National Monument.

Our work on *Topaz* next took us to Russia for visits in their labs and for interviews with Russian nuclear scientists.

We returned one afternoon to the Radisson Hotel in Moscow. There in the lobby, enjoying a happy hour drink with colleagues, was a famous former colleague at CBS News: none other than the late Walter Cronkite. Sitting with him was the late Sandy Socolow, Walter's executive producer for many years.

I remarked to others in the crew that Walter was a professional acquaintance of mine. The crew members didn't know whether to believe me or not. I walked over and reminded Walter that we were former colleagues as earlier chapters of this memoir describe. I introduced the crew members who realized that I was telling the truth. Walter and I traded stories on what had brought us to Moscow—*Topaz* for me and the crew and early discussions on a documentary Walter and Sandy were planning.

I mentioned the joint project on nuclear power for deep-space exploration. Walter remembered an earlier visit to Moscow. His overriding impression fifty years earlier was how backward Soviet technology seemed to be and how poor most of the citizens were. When he landed back in New York at the time, he told an interviewer that the USSR was so backward that the US had little cause for concern about the Soviets' nuclear development, peaceful or otherwise.

The very next day, to his great chagrin, Walter said the *New York Times* printed a story from Moscow that the USSR had just successfully tested its first nuclear device!

Upon my return to Washington, I contacted Walter's son Chip at their production company and asked if Walter might be interested in narrating our *Topaz* documentary. Chip said that his father's current arrangement with CBS forbade him from lending his name to other productions. Nothing ventured, nothing gained. An obscure former CBS News reporter ended up doing that narration—me!

Our crew went to St. Petersburg to do interviews and tour lab facilities. That visit in March occurred with the vernal equinox. One day darkness still came in the late afternoon. The very next evening, the sun did not set until much, much later. The next morning, the sun rose much earlier than the previous few days. The change was a "bright sunshine welcome" with the change to springtime, a stark difference in sunlight the nearer one gets to the North Pole.

I finished the final production of *Topaz* back in Washington. Our American female technical advisor was fluent in Russian. She translated the script into Russian and had a Russian colleague record that version of the program.

As mentioned earlier, our *Topaz* documentary received an honorable mention award at the Charleston (South Carolina) Film Festival, but I know of no other distribution anywhere outside the confines of the State Department or unknown broadcast facilities in Russia. Somewhere, perhaps in some storage facility in an office or a home library, one or more copies may still be gathering dust.

A decade later I would be back in the same State Department assistance office. I was able to fly to Albuquerque for an informal ten-year reunion with Dr. Thome and several of the original Sandia Lab scientists.

My checkered career pattern then took me back to business matchmaking in the private sector, to play roles in environmental oversight and in developing additional sources of electricity Southeast Asia, based in Bangkok. Stay tuned.

THE COUNTRY THAT GAVE UP

With the enormous geopolitical earthquake after the collapse of the former Soviet Union, this is a speech I delivered at my local Toastmaster's Club in Vienna, Virginia. In retrospect, I realize with great humility that I may have been eerily prescient.

Once upon a time, there was a country that decided it had done enough. It had attained greatness as a vibrant new democracy. It had responded to threats to its security and to defend liberty for its closest friends. It had shed blood often, spent trillions of its citizens' tax dollars, and rejoiced in the celebration of many honest-to-goodness heroes. Heroes of both sexes, of many races, from all parts of its land and its territorial possessions.

Friendly Toastmasters, ladies and gentlemen: this great country out-lasted, outsmarted, and outperformed all its enemies. It had won the war of ideas, of men's minds, of human hearts. It was, in a word, the only true superpower, more from its commitment to others than from the might of its national armies. Its very name epitomized universal freedom and justice, more than it did a fixed place on the planet.

Then, with hardly a whimper or whisper, it decided to give up.

The country's national debates became endless bouts of sleaze and gossip and ignored the hallmarks of virtue and industry. Its national level politicians, tranfixed on how the national tax pie was sliced up every year, and always squabbling over which party held power all the way up to the highest job in the land, in a modern day Tower of Babel on a Hill called Capitol.

One party preferred to see the world's strongest economy devastated, merely to improve its chances of winning the Peoples' House. The other party hardly differed and seemed just as intent on getting the goods on rivals, rather than fixing broken programs, broken communities, broken lives.

The nation's avenues, boulevards, and downtown streets in places named for the angels or saints like Francisco and Louis and Paul were overrun with homeless thousands who had given up coping with the vicissitudes of modern urban society. Weaned on a welfare system that awarded aimlessness and robbed self-respect, the country's so-called work force fell into meaningless shouting matches over rights versus responsibilities.

Business executives spent corporate budgets frivolously and toyed with the lives and fortunes of employees, as if no one had emotions or ambitions, dreams, or families.

The nation's public schools were no longer engaged in the exciting task of nurturing and nourishing young minds, instead became stultifying ghettoes where schoolteachers earned wages barely above subsistence level, where unneeded social engineering desires took much higher priority than reading-writing-arithmetic, where children were not challenged but rather reduced to a new low in institutionalized babysitting, and where administrators and school boards lost all sense of leadership.

Immature and ignorant adults more likely preferred to settle foolish arguments by a gunshot or knifing rather than by a handshake or hard-ball debating. Streets in too many neighborhoods in too many cities and towns became cheap and senseless killing grounds. Television commentators showed every bit as much enthusiasm and excitement comparing murder rates around the country as earlier news readers had comparing sports idols' athletic feats and won and lost records.

The favorite pastime turned from baseball and "boy meets girl" into very successful teen suicide. This new national fad became the second largest cause of death among teenagers, where every year a million cases of "boy meets girl" resulted in a million unwanted pregnancies, half a million undesired babies, and another half a million adolescent abortions.

The nation's cities, once beehives of energetic activity around the clock, could not match the overwhelming violence and despair engendered by an avalanche of drugs. Many cities became wretched collections of human flotsam. Social budgets could not cope with the steel vice between reduced revenues and exploding social service needs.

People forgot how to laugh, how to sing, how to play.

The national dream became a surreal nightmare. Few wanted to return to the robust business of solving problems, however large or small they may have been.

The Holy Bible and other foundational teachings of morality lost ground to so many false prophets who guaranteed instant happiness and comfort and dismissed such values as honesty, sacrifice, and persistence. Comparisons with the decadent empires of Babylon and Rome could not have been more striking. Especially evident were the aberrant theories on sexual and gender experimentation advanced by radical poseurs.

No one dared own up to this national failing—NIMBY, Not In My Back Yard—or "It's the other guy's fault". Too many citizens shirked from taking responsibility for the scourge of pessimism and defeat.

Then things began to change. People remembered that a man named Martin, a servant named King, assassinated in the prime of life, had cried out,

> "If America is to be a great nation, the rough places will be made plains, and the crooked places will be made straight, and the glory of the Lord shall be revealed, and all flesh shall see it together. This will be the day when all of God's children will be able to sing with new meaning, "My country 'tis of thee, sweet land of liberty".

People remember that a songbird named Gaye, a gifted man named Marvin, also killed before his time, had asked the questions in his soulful song, *Save The Children*:

> "Who really cares to save a world in despair? There'll come a time, when the world won't be singing, flowers won't grow, and

bells won't be ringing. Who really cares? Who is willing to try, to save a world that is destined to die? When I look at the world, it fills me with sorrow; little children today really will suffer tomorrow. Oh, what a shame. Such a bad way to live. Who is to blame, when we can't stop living?"

People remembered the refrain from a lesser-known group of singers known as the Blue Notes, shouting,

"Wake up everybody, time to build a new land, I know we can do it if we all lend a hand. The world ain't gonna get no better, if we just let it be. The world ain't gonna get no better. We got to change it girl, just you and me."

From the unlikeliest offices of private business, visionary leaders—full of courage and confidence yet despised by the narcissistic intelligentsia—rose up to lead this historic effort.

Voters repudiated the status quo and its chief defenders, those entrenched politicians and "group think" news media who'd lost all sense of fairness and objectivity. Just the threat of term limits produced an army of problem-solvers on Capitol Hill.

Americans rededicated themselves to forming platoons of problem-solvers, reminding themselves like another songbird named Whitney, taken too early from us, had sang, *"Once you know what love is, you never let it end."*

Teachers' salaries shot up, schools were cleaned up and built up. Kids were submerged in fun, yet intensive, learning environments.

Modern-day couch potatoes turned into disciples of doing right. Culprit corporations and inept bureaucracies were penalized and reborn in the best spirit of those early Americans who'd longed for all of us to treasure the beauty of this abundant land.

Problems still persisted, what with the sufferings of opiod addictions throughout the land, and the lost hopes of unambitious minds and bodies. But people just like you and me realized that life has purpose only when problems get our full attention, and solutions our full determination.

The country that gave up—suddenly grew up.

The country that gave up—learned that there is no such thing as a free lunch, that sustaining freedom for everyone, and achieving dreams, have a price.

The country that gave up learned that with faith, energy, love, and undiminished courage, it could become great again.

And it did.

And everywhere the multitudes of the people—on their knees or in silent solemnity—cried out, "To God be the glory. God bless the U.S.A."

"Whoever has ears, let them hear what the Spirit says to the churches." Revelation 3:21

\# \# \#

CHAPTER 26

Combining My Business Activities With My Christian Witness, 1995–Present

"I have told you these things, so that in me you may
have peace. In this world you will have trouble.
But take heart! I have overcome the world"

—John 16:33, NIV.

"Then you will know the truth, and
the truth will set you free"

—John 8:32, NIV.

MY CONSULTANT APPOINTMENT at the State Department terminated near the end of the 1994 year. I reached out to Parallax, Inc., a woman-owned small business specializing in environmental engineering. Its main client was the US Department of Energy, and its role was to help clean up several of the nuclear sites in the US. Its president was a young African-American lady named Margie Lewis. She held a PhD in nuclear physics. Her vice president was Ron Shaffer, a former navy nuclear engineer who had served aboard US Navy nuclear submarines. Ron was a former college athlete. He was a linebacker on the Ohio State Buckeyes football team that won the mythical national championship in 1968.

Ron wanted to explore environmental cleanup opportunities in many of the fast-growing economies Asia. Some cynical observers had labeled some affected countries as sewers for their failure to overcome serious chemical contamination of groundwater, inter alia. My first marketing trip was to talk to business contacts in Taiwan, Hong Kong, Thailand, Singapore, and Indonesia. Within a few weeks, Ron and I were back on the road, with me introducing him to potential partner companies in Thailand, Indonesia, and Singapore. We thought these three were the most promising for environmental cleanup opportunities.

Parallax President Margie Lewis was too impatient and did not wish to spend company budgets developing promising cleanup opportunities. Ms. Lewis also decided against her company pursuing potential work in Indonesia on a national priority in Java to help overhaul key elements of the electricity-generation system. I had lined up excellent and trustworthy local contacts in Thailand and Indonesia to assist Parallax. But she dismissed me as a drain on her company budgets.

Those were very heady days before the currency crisis hit in 1997. Thailand was striving to become one of the new export-oriented economies nicknamed *Asian Tigers*. Demand for electricity all over the region was becoming insatiable with the rush to build more and more export facilities.

Within a year, I was back in Thailand with an electricity development company started by the late John Wing, someone close to me at West Point, from our same 1968-year group. John had opened negotiations with the president of Siam Cement Company (hereafter Siam Cement), Thailand's largest industrial conglomerate. The early discussions were the area of technology transfer to help Siam Cement build up to four power generation facilities. John told his Thai interlocutors that he could build an independent power facility that would generate electricity at slightly lower cost than Siam Cement was paying the national utility.

John thought our West Point roots were fortuitous for his needs, given my background, language fluency, and country familiarity with trustworthy stakeholders.

He was a Baker Scholar at Harvard Business School. After Harvard he went to work for the CEO of General Electric, Jack Welch. Soon thereafter he joined Kenneth Lay, the founder of Enron, where John assumed dual CEO positions for Enron Power and Enron Co-Generation. This was well before the scandals that hit Enron in 2001.

John became a global pioneer in the construction and financing of private power plants, when national utilities in most countries had too many regulations and restrictions that hindered their ability to keep up with demand.

He mentioned to me that his ROI, return on investment, for the Teesside plant he had developed in the UK had been roughly 40 percent on a project costing $1.8 billion. His ROI from that project was in the hundreds of millions of dollars.

John also started his own aviation company, Wing Aviation, providing worldwide private aviation assets for corporate clientele. He obviously was able to use his company's line of Gulfstream executive aircraft whenever and wherever he traveled.

Into this very robust business environment I came, hoping to prove my worth. As the famous quote from David Lloyd George says, "Don't be afraid to take a big step if it's indicated. You can't cross a chasm in two small jumps."

In informal conversations earlier in Washington and in Houston, John told me about his initial talks with Siam Cement. The Thai conglomerate envisioned building up to four power plants near its domestic mining operations, each requiring capital costs of approximately $100 million. His office mentioned that John would be in Thailand in a few days to continue discussions. I took a risk and flew to Bangkok. On the morning he was arriving, I positioned myself in the huge lobby of the world famous Oriental Hotel.

John had no idea I would be waiting personally to welcome him! We had a short discussion in his suite. He not only wanted to have meetings with Siam Cement's CEO but also hoped to see other stakeholders, including key officials in government and executives at the national utility EGAT (Electricity Generating Authority of Thailand). He seemed to be dependent on the Siam Cement CEO to arrange those meetings. I would ensure those meetings happened.

In the space of seventy-two hours on, I took it upon myself to arrange meetings with three key people: the country's minister of industry, who was a twenty-year personal friend; the manager of the national utility EGAT; and the director of the National Energy Policy Office, the son of an acquaintance of mine and former Thai ambassador to the US.

John hired me almost on the spot at a salary that was very sufficient. His company was owned by a major electricity utility, Western Resources, based in Topeka, Kansas. He was able to draw on Western's much larger financial resources for preconstruction of what were called greenfield projects in Thailand, the Philippines, and Indonesia. He had no country manager for Thailand prior to my appearance.

It was a heady time. I proved my value by arranging, quite easily, those important appointments. I showed him that foreign companies like his needed to have additional channels of information on large investments and not to depend entirely on any channels of information suggested by a potential local partner, with unknown ulterior motives. Lacking additional sources of information, John and other foreign business executives were likely to lose valuable leverage in all negotiations and operations.

Within a few days of my return to the US, John named me the Managing Director in Thailand for The Wing Group. God showed that He was answering prayers in many, many ways. I had leaped David Lloyd George's "chasm" with a big step.

Upon my return, John requested I join him two times on short notice, in Boston. The first trip was to discuss current oil and gas industry trends with a well-known energy consultant, Daniel Yergin, President of Cambridge Energy Research Associates, or CERA. I became privy to valuable global forecasts and trends. That overnight trip to Boston allowed me to earn a sizeable stipend from CERA, besides getting access to CERA's continuing research.

The second trip to Boston was to reconnect John with the Thai minister of industry he had just met weeks earlier in Bangkok. The same minister was visiting his son and attending an alumni function at his alma mater, Clark University, in nearby Worchester. The minister agreed to lend what support he could to the project for Siam Cement. Insiders knew that Siam Cement's biggest owner, who held 40 percent of its shares, was the Crown Property Bureau, advocate for and manager of the Thai Royal Family's global investments.

Over the next eighteen months, I traveled often to Bangkok on full expenses, including five-star lodging and business class airfare. I was always looking for ways to help in preconstruction negotiations and escorting and advising Wing Group technical people from Houston and the Vice President for Asia, based in Singapore.

But almost as soon as our development effort started, it collapsed—in a big way. Economies in the region—chiefly those in Thailand, Malaysia, and Indonesia—came under enormous attacks on their currencies from George Soros and his analysis that these countries were investing too much in relatively unproductive assets. One caution was that Thailand had devoted too much investment into golf courses and not enough hard currency in assets such as expanded resource development, updated or new factories.

To Soros, it seemed that these currencies were overvalued. He placed huge bets against them. Overnight, the Thai baht lost about 50 percent of its value against hard currencies. The exchange rate went from twenty-five baht to the dollar to nearly fifty baht to the dollar. The fast-paced, region-wide boom in all types of construction dried up quickly. Commercial property developers went bankrupt; projects under construction came to a halt. "White elephants" started popping up all over the capital cities of Kuala Lumpur, Jakarta, and Bangkok: unfinished commercial and residential real estate.

In Bangkok, hundreds of building cranes disappeared from the skyline. Myriad companies became insolvent. Suicides increased. Many employees in the financial services sector were forced into very low-paying enterprises, such as making sandwiches at home and selling them on Bangkok streets. Vast numbers of citizens returned to their home provinces to take up farming or explore other ways to make a living. Informal weekend markets popped up in the Thai capital. Owners of luxury automobiles, private airplanes, and other ostentatious outlays of wealth hoped to regain relatively few pennies on the dollar. Misery was the daily diet for millions of citizens in a truly boom to bust environment.

Our partner Siam Cement was not spared. Because of its size and prestige everywhere from its relationship with the Thai Royal Family through the Crown Property Bureau, the corporation had dismissed the need to hedge its foreign currency debt. Like hundreds of businesses in the country, the conglomerate had to take emergency measures to continue operations. A small private developer like The Wing Group would have been rejected immediately by any international bank if seeking project financing for a client that was technically bankrupt.

Other energy developers also limped through most of 1998. Western Resources terminated its funding of The Wing Group, putting an enormous strain on John. At Christmastime, he announced that he was giving all employees three months of severance pay but closing the company in January.

Winston Churchill is quoted as saying that the definition of success is going from failure to failure without any loss of enthusiasm. For me, I was succeeding too well: failure seemed to have become commonplace. Suddenly, my risk-taking seemed foolhardy and dangerous.

The three months of severance pay was very welcome, but I needed to locate income opportunities to support my family. For the immediate future, nothing seemed likely in Asia. I had to turn my focus back to domestic opportunities, but the Asian currency crisis had a negative tangential effect in many advanced economies. Russia suffered a massive devaluation of the ruble in its own banking crisis and defaulting on sovereign debt.

Then our family received sad news. Doctors had misdiagnosed my mother's ill health as some sort of heart condition. By the time the correct diagnosis of pulmonary fibrosis was confirmed, it was too late. Her lungs were filled with abnormal fibrous growth that robbed her of almost all her lung capacity. Nearly every breath became a difficult endeavor. As she lay helpless in a hospital bed, tied to a machine to help her breathe but forced to wheeze every few seconds, my father made the heartbreaking decision to terminate her life support. She passed away the night before Palm Sunday at the relatively young age of seventy-eight.

The biggest support pillar for me in those years was, and would continue to be, my belief in the promises of a loving heavenly Father. I remembered the words of Isaiah 55:8–11.

> [8] "For my thoughts are not your thoughts, neither are your ways my ways," declares the LORD. [9] "As the heavens are higher than the earth, so are my ways higher than your ways and my thoughts than your thoughts. [10] As the rain and the snow come down from heaven, and do not return to it without watering the earth and making it bud and flourish, so that it yields seed for the sower and bread for the eater, [11] so is my word that goes out from my mouth: It will not return to me empty, but will accomplish what I desire and achieve the purpose for which I sent it."

I would be remiss if I did not mention a major spiritual experience a few years before the energy development effort in Thailand. I read about a national UMC ministry called *The Walk to Emmaus*. That effort grew out of the post–World War II movement begun by Roman Catholic soldiers in Spain to help reduce the horrors of world wars, by stimulating church renewal. *The Walk to Emmaus* was derived from *Cursillo de Cristiandad*, meaning a short course in Christianity. Anther similar international ministry was *Tres Dias*.

I asked my lay-speaking director Billy Chapman about it. He was a veteran of the spiritual walk and agreed to sponsor me on the three-day weekend. The timing was inconvenient for me. Billy told me not to worry: each person going on the walk would go at the perfect time for him or her, and to erase any worries about delays. I tucked that away for later consideration.

I was able to attend the walk the following year (1997) before the business assignment with The Wing Group. Billy was unable to continue as my sponsor and turned me over to a close friend of his and fellow Methodist lay speaker and Emmaus veteran, Phil Hannum.

Readers are welcome to learn more about the weekend on their own. For me, and probably many others, it was certainly a mountaintop experience, conducted at a 4H facility snuggled in the Blue Ridge Mountains outside Front Royal, Virginia. The weekend is conducted by a cadre of up to two dozen Emmaus veterans and with pastoral supervision from two or three ordained pastors.

There are fifteen short talks on various aspects of Christianity; veterans in the cadre give more than half of the talks. Plenty of singing, praying, and sharing communion takes place, along with many other acts of Christian love and introspection. *The Walk to Emmaus* concludes on Sunday evening. Pastors and cadre admonished us that going back down from the mountaintop to the normal routines would test our new spiritual standing. Two Scripture passages come to mind about descending back to daily routines from any mountaintop experiences. "The shepherds returned (to their fields), glorifying and praising God for all that they had heard and seen, as it was told them." Luke 2:20 (NKJV) and "For the Lord has not given us the spirit of fear, but of power and of love and of sound mind." 2 Timothy 1:7 (NKJV)

Hopefully we would inspire others to become more purposeful in following Jesus.

The Walk to Emmaus became a natural reinforcement to lay speaking, the former an intense short course "on steroids" after nearly a decade of substitute preaching, serving, and leading worship as a lay speaker. The pastors and cadre also encouraged us to volunteer to serve on the cadre in any future walk. All those who did their first walk, men and women, were strongly encouraged to serve on the cadre in any future walk. No one was allowed to repeat the walk as a novice.

My friendship with Phil Hannum deepened through weekly small group meetings and various other events. Two years later, I served as a surrogate father of the bride in his marriage to his Japanese-American fiancé, Kimiko. She was a veteran of the ladies walk and a strong believer. That marriage took place under authority of the West Jersey Grove Association at Malaga Camp, near Vineland, New Jersey. Malaga Camp was a semipermanent community of Christian believers, offering two weeks of customary camp meeting and evangelists every summer. Phil and Kimiko owned one of the small cottages.

The deep spiritual friendship extended by Phil and several other *Emmaus* men and women, especially during monthly dinners and worship, led me to apply for the cadre for the first of two men's walks in 2000. My application was quicky accepted.

Volunteer cadre members commit to approximately eight weeks of training on Saturday mornings. After the first two weeks of self-discovery and sharing of testimonies, the pastors leading the walk make assignments for servant positions and speaking assignments among the volunteers.

I was selected to give the talk entitled *A Life of Piety*. Other smaller roles were also handed out and practiced or learned in the remaining weeks of preparations.

For that first walk in 2000, I recruited several novices for the men's and women's weekends, including my now widowed father, our local church pastor and wife, and three others.

The modern-day *Walk to Emmaus* is based on Luke 24, the biblical event immediately after the crucifixion of Jesus Christ. That passage (from the NIV) beginning with verse 13 says:

> [13] Now that same day two of (his followers) were
> going to a village called Emmaus, about seven miles from

Jerusalem. [14] They were talking with each other about every-thing that had happened. [15] As they talked and discussed these things with each other, Jesus himself came up and walked along with them; [16] but they were kept from recognizing him. [17] He asked them, "What are you discussing together as you walk along?" They stood still, their faces downcast. [18] One of them, named Cleopas, asked him, "Are you the only one visiting Jerusalem who does not know the things that have happened there in these days?" [19] "What things?" he asked. "About Jesus of Nazareth," they replied. "He was a prophet, powerful in word and deed before God and all the people…

[25] He said to them, "How foolish you are, and how slow to believe all that the prophets have spoken! [26] Did not the Messiah have to suffer these things and then enter his glory?" [27] And beginning with Moses and all the Prophets, he explained to them what was said in all the Scriptures concerning himself. [28] As they approached the village to which they were going, Jesus continued on as if he were going farther. [29] But they urged him strongly, "Stay with us, for it is nearly evening; the day is almost over." So he went in to stay with them. [30] When he was at the table with them, he took bread, gave thanks, broke it and began to give it to them. [31] Then their eyes were opened, and they recognized him, and he disappeared from their sight. [32] They asked each other, "Were not our hearts burning within us while he talked with us on the road and opened the Scriptures to us?"

Organizers of the *Emmaus* weekend wanted it to be a powerful and inspirational encounter through continuous Christian love that was showered upon all the novices. No wonder it is described quite correctly as a mountaintop experience.

I had also been assigned to be a table leader for that walk, where novices are divided into small groups to sit together. The table leader becomes the closest cadre member for each novice during the weekend. Bonds form quickly between the leader and his table mates.

The longest friendship I have formed with any novice from that table has been with Jon Moeller, a former FBI agent. For many years as a senior FBI agent, he was stationed in my hometown of Sioux City. Our mutual love for baseball drew us together: I a lifelong St. Louis Cardinals fan; he a fan of the Kansas City Royals. His club defeated mine in the only World Series featuring both in 1985. We remain close brothers in the Lord to this day.

Within a few months, I persuaded our children to attend *Chrysalis*, the high school version of *the Walk to Emmaus*. The entire *Emmaus* model is modified for teenage novices. The most important question I wanted answered was whether or not Donnie and Vanessa believed sincerely that Jesus Christ is the Son of the Living God and God incarnate.

Adult cadre on the team assured me that Donnie and Vanessa swore such belief in Jesus Christ as Lord and Savior. Scripture says, "I have no greater joy than to know my children are walking in truth," per 3 John 4 (NIV)

I joined the men's cadre for the *Walk to Emmaus* again the next year. I recruited and sponsored a few adults from my home church, to include two wives for the women's walk. I was again asked to present one of the several talks to the male novices, besides other serving opportunities. I was not selected as a table leader.

A few months later, and just before 9/11, I was bothered by some errant theology affecting our local church. I resigned from the church and began looking for nearby churches of other denominations. I began to attend another nearby church, Calvary Church of the Nazarene in Annandale.

The church was of comparable size to our family's former UMC church but with a much better music ministry and much stronger exegetical preaching. I asked Donnie and Vanessa to begin making friends among the youth group at Calvary. The youth ministers at Calvary were impressed with the level of biblical knowledge and spiritual maturity that both children showed. I revert to the Scripture quoted above on having no greater joy than to know my children walk in truth.

My wife still shied away from converting to Christianity but enjoyed meeting several ladies at the new church. I joined the choir and participated in two small groups at Calvary.

The pastor at Calvary left two years later. He was promoted to the position of superintendent for all Nazarene churches in Virginia. The incoming pastor was not seminary-trained. His preaching was disappointing. Our family began drifting away. I began looking for a stronger Bible-based church.

Vanessa would unknowingly lead the way, through her own musical talents and her fluency since high school in American Sign Language. She was disillusioned like me with the change of pastors at Calvary. When she returned from college for Christmas vacation and during the summers, she joined the young adult choir and the ministry for deaf attendees at McLean Bible Church, an independent megachurch within a few miles of our home.

I went along with her one Saturday in December to distribute food in the poorer section of Washington. I enjoyed the opportunity. The next Sunday morning I attended the weekly service at McLean Bible Church to informally evaluate its adherence to biblical preaching, inter alia.

The church itself was started four decades earlier by four families who desired a strong Bible church in the Virginia suburbs. When Vanessa was becoming active, the church was experiencing enormous growth. A few years earlier the church bought the property and huge headquarters building of the National Wildlife Federation building close to the business and commercial hub of Tysons Corner.

Much of the church's phenomenal growth was due to its famous pastor, a Messianic Jew who grew up in the Tidewater area of southern Virginia. Lon Solomon began his college studies at the University of North Carolina. He openly admitted to experimenting with marijuana and comparing world religions outside Judaism when he accepted Christ. Lon said he was converted to Christianity in Chapel Hill by a street preacher named Bob Eckhart.

By the early 2000s it was attracting more than ten thousand worshippers on weekends, hosting five weekend services at its main campus and opening satellite campuses in other DC-area locations. It became the largest church in the mid-Atlantic and, to oversee scores of ministries, the church employed a full-time staff of more than three hundred lay and ordained employees.

After a few weekends of evaluation, I applied for membership, I began serving in several of the ministries, honoring my daughter's insights in making McLean Bible Church her new home.

But like both my previous churches, Graham Road United Methodist and Calvary Church of the Nazarene, McLean Bible Church has suffered from an even more unusual change of management. As of this writing, the church has become a victim of a quiet coup in helping orchestrate Lon Solomon's retirement. The coup was led by the new extremely liberal faction of the Southern Baptist Convention, with shameful assistance from longtime church elders and internal employees.

At this writing, legal proceedings are proceeding. Disgruntled plaintiffs among church members charge that the new regime violated the church constitution: that the church's very founding document stated that it would always be independent and never belong to any denomination. All of these unpleasant events continue to this day.

# # #

## CHAPTER 27

Final Thoughts About Following Christ and My Dad

"Enter ye in at the strait gate: for wide is the gate,
and broad is the way, that leadeth to destruction,
and many there be which go in thereat: Because
strait is the gate, and narrow the way, which
leadeth unto life, and few there be that find it"

—Matthew 7:13–14, KJV.

"Do not be deceived: God cannot be mocked. A man
reaps what he sows. Whoever sows to please their flesh,
from the flesh will reap destruction; whoever sows to
please the Spirit, from the Spirit will reap eternal life. Let
us not become weary in doing good, for at the proper
time we will reap a harvest if we do not give up. Therefore,
as we have opportunity, let us do good to all people,
especially those who belong to the family of believers"

—Galatians 6:7–10, NIV.

JUST LIKE MY church hopping, my business career experienced significant changes. As the saying on a Christian radio station goes, "If you don't like adventure, the life of faith is not for you."

The extraordinary currency crises in 1998 in Southeast Asia and in Russia not only caused me financial hardship. It led to thousands upon thousands of business and banking failures, severe unemployment, and mental distress in many countries.

I kept up my attendance at our men's weekly Bible study. My volunteering to serve as a cadre member on two *Walks to Emmaus* deepened my desire to serve Christ. I was very proud that my father was a novice on the walk in 2000, a year after the loss of my mother, his life partner for fifty-eight years. I prayed frequently that he be blessed every bit as much as I had been on my novice walk before him.

Dad built upon that spiritual experience by proposing marriage to a second wife, JoAnn Nelson. Her family was close to ours. We all had attended the same church in Sioux City. JoAnn and my mother had been dear Christian friends in numerous church activities. At the time of Dad's proposal for marriage, JoAnn had been widowed for nearly thirty years.

In mentioning their courtship, Dad repeated over and over the admonition in James 1:27: "Religion that God our Father accepts as pure and faultless is this: to look after orphans and widows in their distress and to keep oneself from being polluted by the world." (NIV)

They were married in Sioux City three months after that 2000 *Walk to Emmaus*. The wedding was officiated by our former pastor there, Richard Pearson, and included many wonderful moments during that weekend. The wedding party consisted of me as best man and both of my sisters, Carole and Cathy, and JoAnn's daughter, Nancy, as bridesmaids. We traveled from different domiciles to be with Dad and JoAnn.

Within a few weeks, I was called back into the State Department, where I served three more years, at first as a speechwriter and special projects' consultant to Deputy Secretary Armitage. Immediately after 9/11, I transferred to the public affairs offices of two regional bureaus, South Asian Affairs and European Affairs.

My most memorable short-term assignment was to escort four foreign reporters to Uzbekistan. They applied to report under State Department auspices on a unique turnover of "excess medical equipment" from US military hospitals in Europe to medical facilities in the New Independent States. One of the reporters was an ethnic Uzbek journalist for the Voice of America. She became a valuable translator during the time our small group was in Uzbekistan.

The turnover of excess medical equipment was a legacy program from 1992. Each year the American military services in Europe would determine which military medical equipment had become obsolete because of newer medical instruments and devices that were being incorporated into the military medical system. Such older equipment was legally declared as "excess to continuing medical needs" and was turned over to hospitals throughout the former Soviet Union.

Many of us working on the assistance program at any time after 1992 had observed that medical care in the former Soviet Union, especially for common citizens, was limited and quite backward. My temporary duty assignments a decade earlier had taken me to primitive healthcare facilities in Russia, Armenia, and Ukraine. Doctors were forced to work without modern types of diagnostic equipment; gauze bandages were used over and over again after repeated washings; and abortion as a form of birth control was widespread. Some mothers reported having ten or more abortions during childbearing years.

Doctors and medical staff in many places in the former Soviet Union enthusiastically welcomed the receipt of such next-to-new equipment.

The city in Uzbekistan chosen for the 2002 transfer was Fergana City, in the heart of the Fergana region approximately 250 miles east of Tashkent. The entire region was much closer to Kyrgyzstan than to Tashkent.

After landing in Tashkent, we boarded buses along with US military personnel chosen to install the medical equipment and give initial training to hospital personnel. The program throughout the entire former Soviet Union has always been an unbelievably meaningful one for the recipients in the numerous hospitals.

These American military personnel stayed in a no-frills hotel in Fergana City. Our small team, however, four reporters and two of us from the State Department, had the relative luxury of staying in something similar to an Uzbekistan Airbnb: a private home with several bedrooms to accommodate customers. The proprietress was an ethnic Russian with Slavic features, including blonde hair, not central Asian facial features and dark hair.

She claimed that her grandparents had endured a forced march from Moscow after the Russian Revolution. The Russian rulers organized forced movements after 1917 as vanguards to establish pro-Communist populations in many new Soviet Socialist Republics like Uzbekistan. Her family moved to Fergana City to distance themselves from politics and engage in crop-growing in the lush valley which had a much different topography from the arid landscape closer to Tashkent. The Tien Shan mountain range separates both parts of the country.

The proprietress spoke better than average English. Her small domestic staff ensured that the residence was up to modern standards in meals, bedding, and overall cleanliness. When we checked out the morning of our departure, our small group collected a gratuity for the service she had provided. She was overcome by our generous gratuity, larger than she expected. She quickly choked up. Tears came to her eyes as she gave me a big Russian hug and said *Dasvidanya* to us, the formal way of saying goodbye.

Allow me to return to my father's second marriage and their new quality of life for nearly a decade in Midland, Michigan. The new partners would pass away within six months of each other: JoAnn from a bad heart in November 2008 and Dad from natural causes in May 2009, only days before his 93rd birthday. Their journey to the Promised Land has preceded mine.

I delivered the eulogy for my father, as I had for my maternal grandparents and my mother: the first eulogy, for my maternal grandfather, in

1991. My dad lived to within days of his ninety-third birthday; my maternal grandfather was almost as old, at ninety-one.

Some of that eulogy follows—dedicated to the very best role model in my life.

> Dad was born in the low-lying rich farmland of southeastern Iowa. As a Son of the Heartland, he lived first in What Cheer, and then Oskaloosa. After high school, he struck out for the big city—Des Moines—where he hired on with Herman M. Brown Company. While in Des Moines, he met and fell in love with Claire Peters, a sassy prairie girl born in the Black Hills of western South Dakota before her family moved to the tiny farm town of Nemaha in northwest Iowa. Within five months of marriage in 1941, the Japanese Navy staged their surprise attack on Pearl Harbor. Dad enlisted in the navy and went to sea in the western Pacific aboard the USS *Starlight*, a troop carrier and transport.
>
> Upon his discharge from the navy and return to Des Moines, the Herman M. Brown Company transferred him to Sioux City. Dad lost his parents at a fairly early age: he was under forty when his father died and under fifty when his mother died.
>
> Dad became one of the "go-to guys" at our home church: among other activities, he was its part-time janitor for more than a dozen years. I spent many Saturdays as a child and teenager sweeping the floors, cleaning the pews, and straightening hymnals for my dad. His lifespan was longer than both his parents. He lost his first wife and my mother after fifty-eight years of marriage; his second wife, after eight years.
>
> Dad was wherever his family needed him to be. He was an assistant coach for our Little League baseball team.

He spent hours helping our junior drum and bugle corps practice at the American Legion hall downtown or at the neighborhood park every summer when we were learning our competitive drill routine.

He loved to hunt and fish with his best friend, Bill Klas. Both of them and their wives loved golfing during the summer in Couples Club. In cooler weather he was a steady teammate on his local bowling team.

And he was a dreamer. One morning he woke up and told my mother he had dreamed of riding a bicycle all the way to Denver. He could not figure out why his legs were so sore, and why the bed was one huge mess of tangled-up bed sheets! He once dreamed he was having lunch with Burt Reynolds. But my favorite was the time he dreamed he and Bill Klas were in Bill's backyard and digging through the earth to reach China. Ten feet down, they hit a solid core of peanut butter!

Dad was wherever his family needed him to be. He and my mother were frequently in Denver, whenever there was a happy event or an unpleasant setback in Carole's family. Just as frequently, he and my mother were in the Twin Cities—whenever Cathy asked them to visit, either before or after Cathy's marriage to Mike Tikkanen in 1991. Both my parents dropped everything they were doing in 1986 and rushed to Virginia to help when Vanessa was born five weeks prematurely and suffering serious neonatal problems for ten days at Children's Hospital in Washington.

When he wasn't driving all those miles or flying to see us, he was on his knees in prayer for hundreds and hundreds of hours. He always wanted the best of things for his family and others around him.

These are the marks of a great man, always available for his family and always proud of all of us. Two proud grandsons carry his name—Donald Dean Thorpe and Donald Marvin Hatcher.

Dad exemplified the fruit of the Holy Spirit: love, joy, peace, patience, kindness, goodness, faithfulness, gentleness, and self-control—against which there is no law (Eph. 5:22–23). I regret how often I may have disappointed him.

The last few days before his passing saw Dad go downhill quickly. For him, he had already laid up his treasures in heaven. Like his beloved first wife ten years earlier, he was headed to the Promised Land, the heavenly paradise with no tears, no disappointments, no troubles, no more death, no sorrow, no crying, no pain. He followed the wise advice of the missionary Jim Elliot, who said as he was martyred in 1956, "He is no fool who gives up what he cannot keep to gain what he cannot lose." What all believers in Jesus cannot lose: the twin gifts of salvation and eternal life. He was a *TFOJ: a True Follower of Jesus.*

Dad's name can be found in the Lamb's Book of Life. Oh, that our names have been written in the Lamb's Book, and that we may ascend to the same destiny.

In the words of the great contemporary Christian song *Because He Lives:*

And then one day, I'll cross that river,
I'll fight life's final war with pain.
And then as death gives way to victory,
I'll see the lights of glory, and I'll know He reigns!

Donald Edward Hatcher was a great man and a great father. Like me, a Son of the Heartland. He has already taken up residence in the Promised Land.

# # #

CHAPTER 28

My Personal COVID Scare. Or Something Else?

"A Visit from St. Nicholas,"

—Clement Clarke Moore, 1779–1863

"'TWAS THE NIGHT before Christmas, when all through the house Not a creature was stirring, not even a mouse."

Nearly every American, and indeed the majority of the world, was affected in some way by the scare and numerous deaths from the COVID-19 virus. I had my own adventure.

Two nights before Christmas 2020, I couldn't fall asleep. Unlike the folks in Clement Clarke Moore's poem, I had not settled down for a long winter's nap.

There was good reason for my unease. Earlier that afternoon, I found myself breathing heavily with every few steps I took around the house, with no idea why. I had to bend over every few steps, just to catch my breath. My lovely wife Vasana sensed something wrong; she forbade me from moving the furniture to help her vacuum the carpets.

The first full year of COVID-19 was coming to a close. I recalled the three tell-tale symptoms of contracting COVID: 1) husky, prolonged, and raspy cough; 2) fever or chills; and 3) extreme shortness of breath, the symptom that fit me. (I would soon learn that the medical acronym SOB was "Shortness of breath".)

My wife drove me to two separate pharmacies that afternoon, one of which had a "drive-through" line for being tested for COVID. Since I had not registered beforehand, I wasn't allowed to be examined.

At home I went online to request an appointment to get tested for COVID-19. The process to register with a primary care physician was still bureaucratic and nearly unworkable. I decided to attempt to register the following day, Christmas Eve.

I never took that step.

I lay in bed that night, bothered by the strangest feeling: a virtually painless warning, so strong that I stood up and walked up and down the hallway outside our bedroom. The Holy Spirit, for sure, telling me to get to the hospital.

I roused my wife and had her drive me to the nearest emergency room, at INOVA Fairfax Hospital, three miles from home.

I would not return home for six days. I spent Christmas Eve and Christmas Day in the care of a variety of doctors and nurses and other medical professionals at INOVA Fairfax Hospital.

THAT LONG NIGHT IN THE EMERGENCY ROOM

I walked up to the Emergency Room reception desk. The staff efficiently took my information and noted my symptom of an extreme shortness of breath (SOB). An ER nurse had me take some steps back and forth to judge my overall physical condition. She led me to a bed in a large temporary ward. It was after midnight when I was wheeled into the ER, past an assortment of beds and medical professionals caring for other patients. It seemed to be a very busy night. I was placed in a private room, probably one that had just become available.

A month later in another ER at the VA Medical Center in Washington, DC, I concluded that the most beautiful people in the world are those who work in Emergency Rooms everywhere in the world. They not only see everything in terms of health problems of all kinds, at all hours of the day and night, but also work tirelessly, sometimes on their feet for hours without stopping, to provide any level of care needed, even in life-threatening situations.

A Registered Nurse named Todd Lange took over. He quickly started to assess my situation. For the next three or four hours, he was absolutely terrific: in many ways, a lifesaver, from the symptoms I was demonstrating. He took time out briefly once or twice to call and update my wife and ask her about my overall health.

The COVID-19 test proved negative. My next visitor was not a healthcare professional per se but an experienced finance officer working the overnight shift and charged with determining my insurability. I was able to prove my Medicare Part A insurance and my Veterans Administration health coverage. I came to understand the need for these finance people to aggressively judge the insurability of all incoming ER patients, even during overnight hours.

The bills coming in during the next several days wold exceed thirty thousand dollars. Fortunately, all charges for the next six days would be covered completely. It was definitely a major relief.

RN Lange maintained his perfect, deliberate, conscientious bedside manner and began to isolate the exact reasons for my SOB and all accompanying symptoms.

At one point, I lost control of my bowels in what was termed *melena*. I leave to readers to learn what *melena* means. RN Lange determined that I had a serious "GI-bleed"—gastrointestinal bleeding, coming almost certainly from a small ulcer somewhere in my stomach or intestines. The SOB was not coming in any way from COVID, but rather was caused by atrial fibrillation from the stress inherent in the GI bleeding.

The next sensation was from what I learned was a TIA—a transient ischemic attack—basically, a mini-stroke with aphasia. *The American Heritage Dictionary* defines aphasia as "partial or total loss of the ability to articulate ideas or comprehend spoken or written language, from damage to the brain from injury or disease". The hospital records early that morning said, "Pt (Patient) is confused and with expressive aphasia... Pt (is) able to follow commands but unable to answer questions properly and is having trouble finding his words."

In short, I did not like someone talking about a "mini stroke". I could not answer RN Lange's simplest questions. Basically, I had an inexplicable failure to answer the easiest questions, such as "What is your primary doctor's name?" or "What street is your doctor's office on?" I was laughing inside over my inability to speak at all.

One of the questions RN Lange asked my wife was any behavior over the last few months that seemed to be amnesia. She said, "Absolutely not," and related how she thought I was completely normal. She told the nurse that I had always had an excellent memory lasting forty years.

Postcript: A very close friend of mine suffered a major stroke in 2023 and now has longterm aphasia. I cannot imagine being (almost?) without hope from losing the ability to speak intelligently for months and years.

RN Lange told me that the ER doctors were going to admit me to the hospital to continue tests and work to overcome the trio of symptoms: the GI-bleed; the aphasia from the TIA/mini stroke, and the SOB that was actually atrial fibrillation caused by the stress from the GI-bleed.

I was cleaned up for the umpteenth time and wheeled out of the ER and up to a private room.

Dawn had already broken. I was in a bed in a hospital room. It was Christmas Eve.

THE CALM ALL ALONG

Whether it was RN Lange's superb professional care in those early morning hours of Christmas Eve, or adjustments my body was making to the various fluids and medicines being administered, I spent my time reflecting and praying often. Sleep was impossible. I remember reciting several favorite

Scripture verses. Even with the aphasia, the GI-bleed, and the atrial fibrillation, I had no major panic or fears. I credit such powerful reassurance as coming from the Holy Spirit. Obviously some relief came from sedatives supplied by all caregivers.

In those few dramatic hours, I repeated over and over the lyrics of Ryan Stevenson from his great 2016 song, *In the Eye of the Storm*, especially the refrain,

> *"In the eye of the storm, you remain in control.*
> *In the middle of the war, you guard my soul.*
> *You alone are the anchor, when my sails are torn.*
> *Your love surrounds me, in the eye of the storm."*

In an interview for *Old Time Music* in 2023, Stevenson told interviewer Corey Hoffman,

> *"The phrase 'In the Eye of the Storm' symbolizes finding peace and tranquility amidst chaos and turmoil. It represents the ability to stay calm and centered in the midst of life's challenges, relying on faith and resilience to navigate through difficult times."*

That perfectly defined the emotions I was feeling throughout those early morning hours. From the discovery of the bleeding somewhere in my stomach or intestines, to the TIA and aphasia, and soon, the doctors' diagnosis of an idiopathic atrial fibrillation, I seemed to handle the ups and downs with tranquility, even serenity.

Now the connection between the diagnoses became clearer.

And the culprit in all this was none other than … Dave Hatcher. Doctors said the GI-bleed (an endoscopy would soon find and excise the small ulcer) probably came from the growing ulcer in the stomach lining caused by daily ingestion of low dose Motrin on an empty stomach, instead of a low dose aspirin or acetaminophen. Neither of those have dangerous side effects like low-dose Motrin on an empty stomach.

That growing irritation-turned ulcer led to the atrial fibrillation, and in turn, caused the TIA and aphasia. Two short episodes of vomiting helped RN Lange and ER doctors separate all three troubles.

FROM CHRISTMAS EVE TO THE LONG WEEKEND

Later in the day, two wonderful adherents of "Good Tidings To All, and To All A Good Day" arrived to celebrate Christmas Eve and decorate my room with an ersatz bonsai Christmas tree and short strings of lighting. My beautiful daughter Vanessa and husband Scott brought Christmas cheer to memorialize the verse from Luke 2:11, "For unto you is born this day in the city of David a Savior which is Christ the Lord". Vasana was at home babysitting our nine-month-old granddaughter Elizabeth (nicknamed "Birdie") so that Scott and Vanessa could decorate my spartan room however sparingly. My lovely wife would get the full effect of the well-intended decorations in that hospital room a day later, Christmas Day.

Throughout the next several days, a steady parade of doctors, nurses, and technicians came in to hook me up to monitors, run IV fluids into my arms (sometimes having trouble finding strong enough veins), and monitor vital signs on a monotonous schedule. I learned that the key vital sign the doctors were focused on was the stability of hemoglobin in the blood, to see how soon the bleeding from the stomach ulcer would stop.

I also was being given medicines to attenuate the fibrillation in the heart.

On that Christmas evening, I was wheeled to the MRI facility to judge the effects within my brain of the TIA. (My aphasia thankfully had disappeared before I left the ER. A telephonic consultation by VA neurologists a few weeks later convinced them that the aphasia had been temporary; my brain functions were very normal. Thanks be to God.)

Back to the MRI: my only other previous MRI was in the same INOVA Fairfax Hospital over thirty years earlier, which ER doctors ordered to observe severe headaches I was suffering. Like the TIA this time, that onset of pain was idiopathic. Only acetaminophen was prescribed then.

This time I started to feel better and better from the various medications for the atrial fibrillation and to overcome any nausea. Merry Christmas! I continued to test negative for COVID.

After supper, a young doctor came to say that the MRI proved negative; the neurology team saw no need for urgent attention. I relaxed.

Relaxed to the point of somehow thinking all had gone well for the previous 24 hours. I foolishly regarded that my condition was stable to the point that doctors would likely discharge me within the next couple of hours. Very wrong-headed thinking.

I reasoned that I could save the hospital all the trouble of waiting until the morning to discharge me. I'd self-discharge myself that very evening!

What a fool!

I changed into my civilian clothes and called Vasana and said that the neurology resident doctor had said everything looked normal. I wanted to believe my own stupidity. I extrapolated that my health was completely back to normal. What a fool! Again. I asked to Vasana to get out of bed and drive the short distance to pick me up.

It was close to midnight. I brainlessly figured that I could E&E (Escape and Evade) down the darkened hallway to the nearest elevator, and that no one would see me walking out to the driveway to meet her. What a fool. Stupid is as stupid does, right, Forrest Gump?

But when I opened the door, I quickly realized that right across the hall from my room was… a nurses' station staffed with not one but two nurses, giving me a bemused look as I stood there in my street clothes!

"Where are you going? Can we help you?" one of them asked, as I started to regret my earlier decision to E&E! What a fool. Duh.

"I'm going home," I mumbled and then greatly bent the truth in saying that the doctors (i.e., the neurology resident) had told me that everything now looked normal, and I saw no benefit in extending my stay in such a wonderful facility! What a fool.

Do you see a pattern here?

One or both nurses, perhaps in unison, hid their astonishment and said something to the effect, "You can't leave! This is a HOSPITAL! Go back to your room and get back in bed and we will see you in the morning!"

INTERLUDE

Maybe I might take the opportunity to write a magnus opus on the hundreds of reports by nurses and doctors and hospital staff describing all manner of complete idiocy by fools like me! Hmm. Perhaps a best seller! Readers would hardly believe how foolish so very many patients can be. Want to bet?

END OF INTERLUDE

I surrendered without a whimper, turned around, and with the elevators to freedom just a few steps away, retreated to my room, completely defeated. I changed back into my hospital gown and called Vasana like a beaten puppy and muttered, "I can't go!" I told her that the nurses didn't see things my way and ordered me back to bed before the doctor berates me in the morning. That doctor said nothing that morning, only wearing a huge grin on her face when she saw me!

I could easily have been a real-life contestant in the "Idiot of All Time Award" like George Costanza in an episode of *Seinfeld*:

> *Jerry to George: "You have no idea what an idiot is. But Elaine*
> *just gave me a chance to get out and I didn't take it. This*
> *is an idiot."*

> *George: "Is that right? I just threw away a lifetime of guilt-free*
> *sex, and floor seats for every sporting event in Madison*

Square Garden. So please, a little respect, for I am Costanza, Lord of the Idiots!"

Vasana said she was less than 30 seconds away when my call of regret came. She was mercifully saved from playing the "Wheelman", the accomplice in my crime of desertion from the huge sophisticated hospital.

Over that long, long Christmas weekend, the nurses and medical technicians administered the MRI and two or three CT scans, plus so many checks of vital signs that my arms resembled purple road maps from my wrists to my elbows.

A couple of nights later, my other infrequent and unwanted visitor showed up: gout in not just one ankle, but both ankles, and corresponding pain level.

I started to feel nauseous again. Doctors realized I was having another attack of atrial fibrillation and prescribed medicine to restore normal heart rate and dispatch the gout attack. Until the anti-gout medicine took a few hours to act. I was virtually immobile for the next twenty-four hours from the crystallization of uric acid in both ankles.

I was discharged four days after Christmas, after doctors were satisfied that my good health was largely restored.

And that is how I celebrated the most unusual Christmas in my life.

My reward: the first evening at home with one gorgeous granddaughter who was completely oblivious to my few days of extreme discomfort. Her her younger sister Tippa and her younger brother William would add their own TLC a few years later. Ain't life grand? On the way to The Promised Land.

Author with Birdie, 2020

Author with "Iowa" Birdie, 2021

Author and wife with Birdie and Tippa, 2023

Birdie, Tippa and Baby Brother Liam

Birdie and Baby Brother Liam

AFTERWORD

The eulogy in Chapter 27 for Dad was my fourth in less than twenty years: for my maternal grandparents, Marvin "Poppy" Peters in 1991, step-grandmother Rose Wedeking Peters in 1993, and for my mother, Claire, in 1999, and Dad in 2009. "Honor your father and mother, so that you may live long in the land the Lord your God is giving you" (Exod. 20:12).

I made Jesus Christ paramount in my life in 1988. I relied heavily on the name of Jesus Christ in publicly celebrating each of the four lives. Readers may see a clear separation between my "before Christ" and "after Christ" eras, regardless of my baptism as a youngster in Iowa, an adult who confessed he was a sinner although never renouncing my faith.

But separating the eras as "before Christ" and "after Christ" was as much cultural as it was geographical, between the Eastern and Western Hemispheres and with an awareness of the variety of Asian religions.

Some readers might wonder why I decided to walk away from a relatively enjoyable and lucrative career as a reporter in Asia in a major lifestyle switch: to being a government bureaucrat first and then an international business consultant, without the same ego satisfaction and earning power I had established in Asia. (The egos in American network journalism everywhere in those days were huge, believe me. They presumably still are.)

When I reflect on the same question. I come to the same conclusion. Without leaving Asia, I may have never felt the Humble Hound of Heaven's gentle nudge. "Here I am! I stand at the door and knock. If anyone hears my voice and opens the door, I will come in and eat with that person, and they with me" (Rev. 3:20, NIV).

That passage is similar to Luke 24:

> "When he (Jesus) was at the table with them, he took bread, gave thanks, broke it and began to give it to them. Then their eyes were opened, and they recognized him, and he disappeared from their sight. They asked each other, 'Were not our hearts burning within us while he talked with us on the road and opened up the Scriptures to us?'"
>
> —Luke 24:30–32, NIV).

If I had remained in Asia with a young family, I may have improved my earning power and the comfortable lifestyle, often venturing into many countries to continue my international reporting. I may never have realized the stark difference in living with Christ, and without.

But my life did change, radically. "Then Jesus said to his disciples, 'Whoever wants to be my disciple must deny themselves and take up their cross and follow me. For whoever wants to save their life will lose it, but whoever loses their life for me will find it.'" (Matt. 16:24–25, NIV).

The Christian life is not an easy life, but it is the only life, once you understand the gift of God, the cost, and the unpredictability of refusing His love. "I am the way, the truth, and the life," Jesus said in the famous passage from John 14:6.

In other words, Jesus Christ is the ultimate truth. I repeat, the ultimate truth.

One more thing: there is no such thing in Christianity as "the family plan" or any variation thereof. One cannot be the beneficiary of all His promises just by being a relative of believers or by a close relationship with true believers but without confession of sin and request for forgiveness. The decision needs to be unilateral, sincere, and authentic. The decision with eternal consequences awaits those who remain undecided. Nonetheless, Jesus said, "In this world ye shall have tribulation, but be of good cheer. I have overcome the world!" (John 16:33b, KJV).

The following passages are from the NIV version. You might want to see if you agree with one or more of my statements reflecting on the Scripture passages.

1. I am a precious child of God and co-heir with Jesus Christ. Scripture says, "Yet to all who did receive him, to those who believed in his name, he gave the right to become children of God" (John 1:12a). "Now if we are children, then we are heirs—heirs of God and co-heirs with Christ, if indeed we share in his sufferings in order that we may also share in His glory" (Romans 8:17).

2. Likewise the Bible teaches that my eternal destiny—eternal— awaits me in Heaven. I have laid up my treasures in Heaven "where moth and vermin do not destroy and where thieves do not break in and steal" (Matthew 6:20).

3. Scripture commends us that "I will praise thee; for I am fearfully and wonderfully made" (Psalm 139:14a). I have already been forgiven for all my sins (1 John 1:9) and cleansed of all unrighteousness. Thanks be to God.

Will you answer His call in a similar way to "Here am I. Send me?" Or will you dwell to some extent and obey as best you can these lyrics by the late A.B. Simpson, founder of the Christian and Missionary Alliance denomination, *Say, Is It All for Jesus?*

Say, is it all for Jesus,
As you so often sing?
Is He your royal Master?
Is He your heart's true King?

Has He your heart's affections,
Your being's ransomed powers?
Your thoughts and way and doings,
Your days and all your hours?

Yes, it is all for Jesus,
Low at His feet I fall.
I bring to Him the royal diadem.
And crown Him Lord of all."

Your very own walk of faith—a lifelong adventure—can begin right now if you accept His gift and His call for obedience. And your life, like mine, will never be the same.

"At the name of Jesus, every knee shall bow, on the earth, above the earth, and under the earth, and every tongue confess, that Jesus Christ is Lord"

—Phil. 2:10–11, NIV.

You too, can write your own story, On the Way to the Promised Land.

\#   \#   \#

ABOUT THE AUTHOR

Dave began sharpening his writing craft with required essays at West Point; his military assignment on communist insurgencies in Asia; and his staff work in later years supporting principals in the Department of Defense—bookends to nearly a decade as a foreign reporter for CBS News, *Newsweek* magazine, and the British Broadcasting Corporation. He likes James Michener's historical novels and the late Og Mandino's short novel *The Greatest Miracle in the World*, containing the priceless "God Memorandum". He lives in northern Virginia with his lovely wife Vasana, plus two grown children and three charming grandchildren living nearby.

#   #   #